The Uncollected Dorothy Parker

THE UNCOLLECTED
DOROTHY PARKER

compiled and with an introduction by
Stuart Y. Silverstein

Duckworth

First published in 1999 by
Gerald Duckworth & Co. Ltd.
61 Frith Street
London WIV 5TA
Tel. 0171 434 4242
Fax. 0171 434 4420
e-mail: enquiries@duckworth-publishers.co.uk

Introduction and editorial arrangement
© 1996 by Stuart Y. Silverstein

Offset from the 1996 Scribner edition
by permission of Simon & Schuster Inc.
Design by Brooke Zimmer

ISBN 0 7156 2937 9

A catalogue record for this book is available
from the British Library.

Printed and bound by
Redwood Books Ltd, Trowbridge

Contents

The "Hate Verses"

Introduction

The literary raconteur Alexander Woollcott only intended to fawn over Dorothy Parker when he included the short (eleven-page) but vastly influential profile in his bestselling 1934 essay collection, *While Rome Burns*. "Our Mrs. Parker" was "a little and extraordinarily pretty woman." Her work was "pure gold" that would be celebrated by future generations. She possessed "the gentlest, most disarming demeanor" while she wielded a verbal "dirk which knows no brother and mighty few sisters." Perhaps she was notorious for stalking human prey, but she loved other animals with a visceral passion. As Woollcott famously explained, Dorothy was "so odd a blend of Little Nell and Lady Macbeth," whose weapon was "not so much the familiar hand of steel in a velvet glove as a lacy sleeve with a bottle of vitriol concealed in its folds."

To illustrate this point, Woollcott catalogued many of the droll and often lethal quips that had been attributed to Dorothy over the preceding fifteen years.[1] But if Dorothy was already as widely known for her tongue as for her pen, which she was, in later years

1. It is dangerous to ascribe particular anecdotes or witticisms to Dottie. Many are at least partly apocryphal, or are known in several conflicting accounts (each with its own version of parties and dialogue), but conversation is ephemeral, and it is often impossible to determine just who said what. Dottie's contemporaries were particularly vulnerable: as another celebrated wit, the eminent playwright and director George S. Kaufman, dolefully predicted, "Everything I've ever said will be credited to Dorothy Parker." But Woollcott's profile did create an abiding interest in cataloguing Parkerisms when he related the following anecdotes, among many others:

Dottie was recuperating in a hospital—a.k.a. "Bedpan Alley"—when

Woollcott's list would be considered the essential primary source for the thriving literary cottage industry that ultimately over-whelmed any other public reputation that she could ever earn.

Dorothy was only forty years old when the profile appeared. She had published three collections of popular and well-received poetry. She was a prize-winning short-story writer, an influential literary and drama critic, and she was just then negotiating a lucrative contract to write screenplays in Hollywood. But after "Our Mrs. Parker" she was primarily a marketable commodity of distinct proportions: the tiny woman with the big mouth who knew the gamut from A to B and wrote irreverent reviews that sounded as though she was still at the Algonquin Round Table; the one who also wrote a few poems, short stories, and film scripts whose titles were not quite so memorable as one might presume; the one who survived those abortions and suicide attempts and wretched affairs along the way and whose life often made her want to fwow up.

The ambitious artist was even degenerating into stock literary and theatrical cliché. In 1932, two years before the Woollcott pro-file, Dorothy was the model for "Lily Malone" in Philip Barry's play *Hotel Universe*. In Barry's description, Lily was "able to impart to her small, impudent face a certain prettiness." Also in 1932, Dorothy was "Mary Hilliard" in George Oppenheimer's *Here Today,* which was directed by George S. Kaufman, a former Algonquin colleague with whom Dorothy usually shared a cordial mutual contempt.

Woollcott came to visit. Soon after he arrived she rang a bell. He asked if she was calling for drinks. "No, it is supposed to fetch the night nurse, so I ring it whenever I want an hour of uninterrupted privacy."

When she heard that an acquaintance had hurt herself in London, Dottie assumed the poor woman must have injured herself sliding down a barrister. And if all the girls who attended the Yale prom were laid end to end, Dottie insisted she would not be at all surprised.

Woollcott recalled that the unpopular wife (Mary Sherwood) of a "success-ful playwright" was forever prattling on about her pregnancy. When the baby was born, Dottie sent her a wire—collect: GOOD LUCK, MARY. WE ALL KNEW YOU HAD IT IN YOU.

In 1934, the year the Woollcott piece appeared, "Dorothy" starred as the dowdy "Julia Glenn" in the Kaufman–Moss Hart comedy *Merrily We Roll Along.* Julia was "a woman close to forty. She is not unpretty, but on her face are the marks of years and years of quiet and steady drinking—eight, ten hours a day." Also in 1934, she was the nightclub singer "Daisy Lester" in Charles Brackett's novel *Entirely Surrounded.* Brackett described her as "a tiny, dark figure in a blue dress with peasant embroidery on the sleeves." He even dedicated the book to her. And in 1944, she surfaced again as "Paula Wharton" in *Over Twenty-one,* a play written by the actress Ruth Gordon and again directed by Kaufman.[2] The die was cast. Dorothy Parker was famous for being Dorothy Parker, and that was what she always would be. And in the popular consciousness, she could never be anything more.

Dorothy Rothschild[3] was born, prematurely, on August 22, 1893, in West End, New Jersey.[4] Her mother, Eliza née Marston, was of English ancestry, and her father, Jacob Henry Rothschild, who preferred to be known by his middle name, came from Prussian Jewish stock. Henry was a partner in a prosperous cloak-making firm, and the family lived a comfortable life with servants in an exclusive neighborhood on the Upper West Side of Manhattan.

A month before Dorothy's fifth birthday, she was devastated when Eliza "promptly went and died" on her. Henry quickly found a new wife, Eleanor Lewis, who was in Dorothy's words "crazy with

2. Dottie was not pleased by the sincerest form of flattery: "I suppose that now if I ever wrote a play about myself, I'd be sued for plagiarism." Another time, Dottie met a playwright she thought was appropriating some of her ideas. He said that his next work was a "play against all isms." Dottie: "Except plagiarism."

3. Dottie later confessed: "My God, *no,* dear! We'd never even heard of *those* Rothschilds!"

4. Dottie: "I was cheated out of the distinction of being a native New Yorker, because I had to go and get born while the family was spending the summer in New Jersey, but, honestly, we came back to New York right after Labor Day, so I nearly made the grade."

[presumably Presbyterian] religion." Dorothy later claimed to so dislike her that she could only address Eleanor as "hey, you" because she could not bear to call her Mother. Eleanor died three years later, when Dorothy was still only nine years old. Dorothy later described an implausibly grim existence that included such standard elements as the distant father and the wicked stepmother, but more prosaically, she was the "artistic" child who wrote verses and loved the assortment of dogs that the family had started adopting and quickly spoiling. She retained her love of undisciplined dogs and most other creatures for the rest of her life.[5]

By the time Dorothy was twelve she was four feet eleven inches tall. She was excessively thin and would remain underweight until she was in her twenties, a fact that she would recall nostalgically, and ruefully, in later years. She had a heart murmur. If she intuitively felt isolated from her world, the schools she attended made her feel worse. At a time when a Rothschild was a Jew and was treated accordingly, Dorothy was enrolled first in a Catholic elementary school, where she often had trouble with the nuns,[6] and then in a restricted Protestant high school (her father lied on the application). She left the high school six months later, when she was fourteen, and did not return. During her

5. In later life Dottie had a dog called Woodrow Wilson. Woodrow suffered from what Aleck Woollcott delicately described as a "distressing malady." According to Dottie, the dog *said* he got it from a lamppost. She later adopted an amiable dachshund called Robinson. Robinson was attacked in the street by a much larger dog whose owner claimed that Robinson had started it. Dottie was incredulous: "I have no doubt that he was also carrying a revolver."

Once Dottie brought her dog to a party, where it vomited on the rug. Dottie tried to apologize, or at least explain, to her hostess: "It's the company." Another time her dog relieved itself in the lobby of the Beverly Hills Hotel. The hotel manager scolded her: "Miss Parker, Miss Parker! Look what your dog did." Dottie stared at him: "*I* did it." And she walked away.

Dottie's record with other animals was less commendable, though she once had a parakeet she called Onan. Why? See Genesis 38:9. But on another occasion a friend asked her how he could get rid of his cat. Dottie: "Have you tried curiosity?"

6. She later argued: "Well, how do you *expect* them to treat a kid who saw fit to refer to the Immaculate Conception as 'Spontaneous Combustion'? Boy, did I think I was smart! Still do."

abbreviated education Dorothy learned Latin and French and developed a keen appreciation of literature and poetry, but in later years she avoided admitting that she had never graduated from high school.[7]

After leaving school she moved in with her father for six increasingly grim years. Henry suffered financial reverses, grew ill, and finally died in 1913, when he was sixty-two and Dorothy was twenty. Though he probably bequeathed a small estate to his four children (Dorothy was the youngest), he did leave something: Dorothy later claimed that she had been left penniless.

In 1914, she found work as a dance instructor while she yearned for the literary life. She experimented with light verse and sold a piece to the famously urbane Frank Crowninshield, who had recently been appointed the editor of the new *Vanity Fair* magazine by the publisher Condé Nast. In nine repetitive stanzas, "Any Porch" casually dissected the meandering conversations of banal upper-middle-class women who had reached a certain age. Dorothy was paid twelve dollars for the piece and received her first known credit when *Vanity Fair* published it in September 1915. Perhaps of greater importance, Crowninshield found himself amused by the callow but promising young talent and, at Dorothy's urgent request, found her a ten-dollar-a-week job writing captions at *Vanity Fair*'s sister publication, *Vogue*.[8]

But working for *Vogue* in 1914, and for forty years thereafter, meant working under the exceedingly proper Edna Woolman Chase, who enforced a strict dress code that included white gloves but prohibited open-toed shoes, and maintained a formidably rigorous standard of decorum. For example, when an editor who had attempted suicide returned to work, Mrs. Chase called her in and told her: "We at *Vogue* don't throw ourselves under subway trains, my dear. If we must, we take sleeping pills."

Dorothy was often a deliberately disruptive force who did not

7. Dottie: "The only thing I ever learned [in school] that ever did me any good in after life was that if you spit on a pencil eraser, it will erase ink."

8. More than forty years later, Dottie recalled the exhilaration of landing that first literary job on *Vogue*: "Well, I thought I was Edith Sitwell."

mesh well with the rest of the *Vogue* staff and particularly did not get on with Mrs. Chase.[9] Though Mrs. Chase did try to utilize her talents,[10] even publishing a verse titled "The Lady in Back" in November 1916, and though Dorothy volunteered for several weird experiments, including a risky new process called a permanent wave, they both realized that Dorothy belonged somewhere else. In the fall of 1917, she moved down the hall to Crowninshield's *Vanity Fair*.

She had been submitting poems and verses to *Vanity Fair* for years. None were particularly good: the next three that Crowninshield published, "The Bridge Fiend," "A Musical Comedy Thought," and "The Gunman and the Débutante," had clever moments but still displayed more potential than competence. And one of them could have destroyed her career.

"A Musical Comedy Thought" was published in the June 1916 issue of *Vanity Fair*. It described, with tongue firmly in cheek, a bizarre but popular vaudeville singer who impersonated women both in voice and couture. But then Franklin P. Adams, the distinguished F. P. A. of the *New York Tribune,* got involved. Adams was New York's preeminent columnist. He also dabbled in poetry and published several highly regarded collections of light verse, which included "Baseball's Sad Lexicon," more familiarly known as "Tinker to Evers to Chance." Nearly every day his Conning Tower col-

9. Dottie was astounded, but hardly speechless, the first time she saw the ornate *Vogue* offices: "Well, it looks just like the entrance to a house of ill-fame."

She wrote this caption for an underwear layout: "From these foundations of the autumn wardrobe, one may learn that brevity is the soul of lingerie, as the Petticoat said to the Chemise." That line actually appeared in the magazine, but the proofreaders caught and scrapped her caption for a photograph of a model wearing an expensive nightgown that suggested commercial, as well as romantic, considerations: "There was a little girl who had a little curl, right in the middle of her forehead. When she was good she was very, very good, and when she was bad she wore this divine nightdress of rose-colored mousseline de soie, trimmed with frothy Valenciennes lace."

10. When Mrs. Chase allowed her to write feature stories, Dottie tried to twist the focus to embarrass her subjects, i.e., her piece on interior decoration used a fictional profile that ridiculed an hysterical and flamboyantly homosexual decorator. The piece was titled "Interior Desecration."

umn published submissions from readers who wanted to display their talents publicly, and the gold watch he gave each year for the best poem was one of New York's most valued literary prizes. It was the mighty Adams who, on May 23, 1916, took notice of young Dorothy Rothschild when he started his column with Dorothy's verse:

> My heart is fairly melting at the thought of Julian Eltinge;
>   His vice versa, Vesta Tilley, too.
> Our language is so dexterous, let us call them ambi-sexterous,——
>   Why hasn't this occurred before to you?

Adams followed it with his own devastating response:

> In answer to your plotty little poem, Mistress Dotty,
>   It often has occurred to me, but then,
> I thought it was absurd to steal a notion that occurred to
>   Percy Hammond in the spring of Nineteen Ten.

Hammond, then a *Chicago Tribune* theater critic, had once described Eltinge as "ambisextrous." Both Adams's contemptuous dismissal and Dorothy's reaction to it are lost to history. There appears to be no record of the exchange outside the old Conning Tower clippings, and though there is no evidence that either Dorothy or Adams ever mentioned it again, it must have been a crushing blow to her. She was only twenty-two, with a tenuous hold on an entry-level literary job, and was desperately trying to make a name for herself in that world. Instead, her first substantial public recognition was as a plagiarist, and a notably clumsy one at that.

Dorothy had at least two similar but vastly less serious brushes with Adams in later years. In 1914, Adams had hailed Dulcinea, a popular character in The Conning Tower, with "Dulcy far niente," a pun on the Italian "dolce far niente," loosely translated as "pleasant idleness." Seven years later, in November 1921, Dorothy borrowed it for "Lynn Fontanne," a verse saluting the star of the hit George S. Kaufman–Marc Connelly comedy *Dulcy,* which was based on the same character. Although Adams surely recalled his earlier sally—he had a fabulous memory—he did not publicly comment on her appropriation. But he did preen while writing "To Dorothy Parker" in The Conning Tower, by then in *The* (New York) *World,* on December 18, 1922:

> *You borrowed, about March Seventeen*
> *"The Life and Death of Harriet Frean."*

It is likely that Adams was jocularly comparing the compellingly dreary title character in May Sinclair's *The Life and Death of Harriett Frean,* which had been published earlier that year, and the stock literary figure described in Dorothy's verse "The Drab Heroine," which had appeared in the March 9, 1922, issue of *Life* magazine. But that was all far in the future when, in mid 1916, Dorothy must have felt severely chastened and was fretfully considering her next step.

She probably had been experimenting with free verse for some time before succumbing to her caustic instincts and finding that she enjoyed writing screeds. The result was a piece called "Women: A Hate Song," a broad and extended diatribe listing the alleged faults of her own sex. Dorothy submitted it to Crownin-shield under the name "Henriette Rousseau";[11] he loved it and put it in the August 1916 issue, to great popular enthusiasm. Crown-inshield asked her for more diatribes, and over the next eight years Dorothy produced seventeen more so-called "hate verses" for both *Vanity Fair* and *Life,* skewering, among other targets, husbands and wives, actors and actresses, books, theater, and film. The series spawned numerous of imitators.

That summer, Dorothy fell in love with Edward Pond Parker II, a tall, fair stockbroker of her own age from an old Connecticut Congregationalist family. She may have conducted desultory affairs with similar men before—she always liked athletes with

11. Years later she signed some pieces "Helen Wells," probably a play on "Hell on Wheels."

good (i.e., northwest European)[12] features—but, she admitted forty years later, Eddie was "beautiful." He was also "not very smart. He was supposed to be in Wall Street, but that didn't mean anything."

When the United States entered the First World War in April 1917, Eddie enlisted in the army and proposed marriage. As Eddie's family disapproved of the match, and Dorothy had already distanced herself from her own family, neither side attended the June ceremony. Soon Eddie was off to train to be an ambulance driver.[13] While he was in France, Dorothy kept the home fires burning by writing hate verses about bohemians and slackers who were not pulling their weight in the war effort.

Dorothy finally found a home at *Vanity Fair*. Crowninshield hoped to bring about a revival of Good Taste—it was said that his "mind was cultivated rather than profound"—and his purportedly frothy magazine was one of the most beautiful, yet aesthetically adventurous, publications of that or any era, on the very cusp of the avant-garde. During his first fifteen years there (during the sixteenth year he helped establish the Museum of Modern Art), *Vanity Fair* introduced a blinding array of new talent to the mass American public: "his" writers included Dorothy, Robert Benchley, P. G. Wodehouse, Edna St. Vincent Millay, e. e. cummings, and Aldous Huxley. Crowninshield took particular pride in *Vanity Fair*'s visual "look," which often startled traditional sensibilities. Though he brought artists such as Rockwell Kent, Pablo Picasso, and Miguel Covarrubias to public attention, Crowninshield ruefully observed in 1928 that "the new artists whom we have periodically presented have aroused the greater part of the criticism that *Vanity Fair* has had to combat from time to time." Crowninshield also employed photographers such as Baron de Meyer and Edward Steichen "when their work was branded as wild and absurd."

Dorothy worked as a general editorial assistant for several

12. Years later, she ruefully described her "type": "I require only three things of a man. He must be handsome, ruthless, and stupid."

13. Dottie: "We were married for about five minutes, then he went off to war."

months, but when Wodehouse took a leave of absence Crownin-shield made her New York's only female drama critic. She started her column in the April 1918 issue and, as with the hate verses, she found she often preferred inflicting abuse to tendering praise.[14] She was amusing, she was witty, she was wicked, and she was noticed. People started talking about that devilish Mrs. Parker.

In November the war ended, but Eddie remained in Europe with the occupation forces. Dorothy continued reviewing plays and submissions while Crowninshield looked for a managing edi-tor. He found an apparently prim and reserved twenty-nine-year-old teetotaler who had written some of the looniest pieces Crowninshield had ever read, and eventually offered him the job. On May 19, 1919, Dorothy arrived at work to meet Robert Benchley: he introduced himself to "Mrs. Parker," she extended her greetings to "Mr. Benchley," and they went to work.

A few days later Crowninshield brought in their new "drama edi-tor," with unspecified duties: a young (twenty-three) and astonish-ingly tall (six-foot-seven) veteran of the Canadian Black Watch regiment called Robert Sherwood. If Benchley was reticent, Sher-wood was silent—so quiet, in fact, that he scared his new cowork-ers.[15] It turned out that Sherwood was very shy, and when he finally loosened up, the three quickly became close friends.

All three left the magazine within the next eight months. "I must say we behaved extremely badly," Dorothy admitted later. She and Benchley subscribed to undertakers' magazines and

14. Though most of her reviews were innocuous, there were notable excep-tions. In her very first column, in April 1918, she suggested attending *Girl O' Mine* "if you want a couple of hours' undisturbed rest. If you don't knit, bring a book." As to *The Love Mill,* "I know who wrote those lyrics and I know the names of the people in the cast, but I'm not going to tell on them." *Sinbad,* she concluded, was "produced in accordance with the fine old Shubert precept that nothing succeeds like undress," which was, at least, an improvement over the production whose chorus line appeared to be composed of "kind, motherly-looking women."

15. Dottie warned Benchley that Sherwood was a "Conversation Stopper," i.e., similar to "riding on the Long Island Railroad—it gets you nowhere in particular."

posted diagrams over her desk. They set their own hours, which caused Nast to institute "tardy slips," which caused Benchley to fill one in to explain that he was eleven minutes late in order to save the city from rampaging elephants. When both Crowninshield and Nast were away, Benchley allowed Sherwood to print a fashion prediction that men would soon be wearing jade-trimmed waist-coats and peg-topped trousers. When they were ordered not to talk about their wages, they wrote the relevant numbers on posterboard and wore them around their necks.

In December, Sherwood was fired. In January, Crowninshield told Dorothy that she was no longer needed because Wodehouse was returning. She knew the real reason was that she had offended some prominent producers with her scathing reviews, including some mild criticism of Billie Burke's (Mrs. Florenz Ziegfeld's) performance in *Caesar's Wife*. Prominent producers were also prominent advertisers. "*Vanity Fair* was a magazine of no opinion, and *I* had opinions," Dorothy said much later. Benchley immediately resigned in protest, though he was barely solvent and had to support a wife and two young children. Dorothy called it "the greatest act of friendship I'd known."[16] For all their highly public bitterness, however, all three were writing in *Vanity Fair* a few years later,[17] and Dorothy even published nine verses there in 1926.

In the January 12, 1920, entry in his Diary of Our Own Samuel Pepys, a weekly feature of The Conning Tower, Frank Adams reported to all of New York that "R. Benchley tells me he hath resigned his position with 'Vanity Fair' because they hath dis-charged Mistress Dorothy Parker; which I am sorry for." Adams no longer considered Dorothy the appropriating parvenu of less

16. After leaving *Vanity Fair,* Dottie ran into Nast in the Algonquin lobby. Nast was a notorious libertine, and he asked her to join him on an ocean cruise. She politely declined; then, as soon as he left, turned to the critic Edmund Wilson: "Oh, God, make that ship sink!"

17. For example, both Dottie and Sherwood participated when *Vanity Fair* asked literary celebrities to compose their own epitaphs for the October 1924 issue. Her entry: "Here Lies the Body of Dorothy Parker. Thank God!" At other times she suggested different closing thoughts, including "Excuse my dust," "This is on me," and "If you can read this you've come too close."

than four years before. She was a colleague, even a friend, someone with whom he had something very useful in common: she, along with Benchley and Sherwood and Adams himself, was a member of the celebrated Round Table of the Algonquin Hotel in midtown Manhattan.

The Round Table had started six months earlier, in June 1919, when thirty-five friends and others attended a luncheon celebrating Alexander Woollcott's return from the American Expeditionary Force in Paris, where he had served on the staff of the soldiers' newspaper, *The Stars and Stripes*. Woollcott had been a *New York Times* drama critic before volunteering for the army and, if he had already known Adams before going overseas, they had become comrades in arms during the several months they spent together on the army paper.

Also present was another former *Stars and Stripes* staffer, the frenzied Harold Ross of Aspen, Colorado, who had become a particular friend and antagonist of Woollcott's. Though Aleck took pleasure in baiting Ross, he had also introduced him to Jane Grant, whom Ross would soon marry. Heywood Broun, the eminent columnist, was also there. Broun had worked with Adams at the *New York Tribune* and had also been in France, though as a civilian correspondent. He would continue to work with Adams for most of the next decade at the *Tribune* and then Herbert Bayard Swope's *World*. A few years after the luncheon, Jane Grant and Broun's wife, Ruth Hale, would form the Lucy Stone League, a feminist organization committed to establishing the right of women to retain their maiden names after marriage.[18]

The journalists George S. Kaufman (*New York Times*) and Marc Connelly (*New York Morning Telegraph*) were both from western Pennsylvania and would soon collaborate on some plays. Their first big hit would be the aforementioned *Dulcy*. They did not attend the first luncheon, but were soon core members of the Table. The press agents John Peter Toohey and Murdock Pemberton were at the homecoming, and would both continue to appear

18. Dottie once sent a wire: TO RUTH BROUN FROM DOROTHY ROTHSCHILD.

for several years. The Table would also eventually welcome the novelist Edna Ferber and the inordinately funny comic writer Donald Ogden Stewart. The popular cover artist Neysa McMein, a statuesque advocate of open marriage,[19] was a frequent and appreciated visitor; so were Margaret (Peggy) Leech, who later married *The World*'s owner—a Pulitzer—and then won two Pulitzer Prizes for history, and Margalo Gillmore, a lively young actress who stole Marc Connelly's heart but did not know what to do with it. Two of the most famous reputed members, Swope and Ring Lardner, actually took pains to avoid the lunches, although they often attended the Saturday night poker auxiliary, the Thanatopsis Club.

Most of the people who comprised the nucleus of the Table were similarly situated: they were relatively young, between twenty-five and thirty-five years old; they were from somewhere else (except Broun and, for all practical purposes, Dorothy) but were desperately anxious to be taken for Manhattan sophisticates; they worked in what would much later be called the communications and entertainment industries; they were ambitious; and they were willing to engage in mutual back-scratching for personal benefit. Their critics called it logrolling.

The primary means at their disposal was pure, undistilled wit: wit that was saved up for the next lunch; wit that could be published in the next morning's newspapers, or spoken about at the next day's rehearsals (with reciprocity, of course); wit that could get plays produced, or jobs offered, or newspapers sold. Dorothy was a particularly useful member, though thirty years later she unconvincingly claimed that she "wasn't there very often—it cost too much."[20] But, like so much of her recollection of her past life,

19. Dottie helped a nervous married friend prepare for his first tryst with Neysa, even taking him to the pharmacy to buy condoms. Then he felt compelled to tell her that it was his first infidelity. Dottie: "Oh, don't worry, I'm sure it won't be the last."

20. In a 1959 television interview, during the course of her campaign to revise her role at the Round Table, Dottie quipped that "most of them are dead now, but they weren't too alive then."

it is conveniently incorrect. She had lunch at the Table with some regularity and tended to socialize with the other Algonks the rest of the time. When Noël Coward encountered the same crowd three times in three different places on the same day, he asked, "Don't they ever see anyone bloody else?"

Dorothy preferred to lurk in the background. She liked to think of herself as a refined lady who did not shout, or even raise her voice, like so many of the others. She felt no compulsion to constantly be clever. But when she did have something she wanted to say—usually some understated ferocity—she characteristically delivered it in a low, hesitant, almost diffident murmur,[21] with a deadpan expression that enormously heightened the effect of the words. But for all the protestations that she only intended to deflate the pompous or humble the arrogant, there was such a gratuitous and even gleeful streak of calculated cruelty to so many of her assaults on less articulate victims that there is no reason to believe that her primary motive was anything more than to humiliate or even disgrace people who had done her no harm, just because she was able and was expected to do so.

Eddie returned to New York in August 1919. He had been a heavy drinker before he sailed with his unit (his army nickname was "Spook"), but during the war his alcoholism had spiraled out of control as Dorothy's intake had also steadily increased. It was clear very soon after he came home that Dorothy had lost interest in him. She claimed that he had returned from France with a morphine addiction, which may have been true, and she publicly humiliated him at parties by introducing him as "my little husband" and, when he was absent, by portraying him as the hapless victim of a series of horrible imaginary misadventures.[22] Marc

21. She once said that "a girl's best friend is her mutter."

22. Dottie's able biographer, Marion Meade, catalogued a few: "He almost got run over; he broke his arm while sharpening a pencil; he narrowly avoided plunging into an open manhole while reading The Wall Street Journal." Dorothy also "recalled" the time they had arrived early for a funeral, and Eddie decided to view the remains. As he knelt before the coffin, which was sitting on a conveyor belt to the crematorium, his knee accidentally hit a button. Before they could react, the coffin rolled into the oven.

Connelly recalled that Eddie was "a quiet, pleasant young man who was out of his element. He couldn't keep up with Dottie."

She apparently described the current state of her disintegrating marriage in some of her verses. In January 1922 she seemed willing to try to make it work, as she declared in a poem she published that month, titled "Fragment":

> It is the quest that thrills, and not the gain,
>> The mad pursuit, and not the cornering:
> Love caught is but a drop of April rain,
>> But bloom upon the moth's translucent wing.
> Why should you dare to hope that you and I
>> Could make love's fitful flash a lasting flame?
> Still, if you think it's only fair to try—
>> Well, I am game.

By June she had lost hope. In "Day-Dreams" she listed a series of poignant domestic episodes, but finally concluded:

> If you and I were one, my dear,
>> A model life we'd lead.
> We'd travel on, from year to year,
>> At no increase of speed.
> Ah, clear to me the vision of
>> The things that we should do!
> And so I think it best, my love,
>> To string along as two.

They separated soon after, and with the exception of a failed reconciliation two years later, they lived separate lives before they finally divorced in 1928.[23] Eddie remarried but died of an accidental overdose of sleeping powders in 1933. He was only thirty-nine years old.

23. Dottie recalled that they got the divorce "in Connecticut, where you can get it for roller skating." The night the divorce came through, Dottie and her new boyfriend, John Garrett II, went to Jack and Charlie's Puncheon Club and

After leaving *Vanity Fair,* Dorothy and Benchley rented a tiny[24] triangular office near Times Square in the Metropolitan Opera House studios for thirty dollars a month, where they joked about future plans[25] while trying to figure out what to do. Dorothy found work as drama critic at the literary *Ainslee's* magazine and did freelance work for *The Saturday Evening Post* and *Ladies' Home Journal,* while Benchley wrote advertising copy and, when he could, book reviews for *The World.* In April 1920, Benchley followed Sherwood to *Life,* a sophisticated humor magazine, where he was appointed drama critic. Dorothy started submitting her rhymes there in September, and over the next three years she sold nearly one hundred verses to *Life* and *The Saturday Evening Post.* It was more commerce than art,[26] as she frankly declared in "The Far-Sighted Muse," which appeared in *Life* in March 1922 (and which also displayed the parenthesized aside that had occasionally been used by the nineteenth-century English poet Thomas Hood, one of her favorites):

> *Smile, and the World will smile back at you;*
> *Aim with a grin, and you cannot miss;*
> *Laugh off your woes, and you won't feel blue.*
> *(Poetry pays when it's done like this.)*

She also wrote a few prose pieces for *Life* and other magazines, but not as many as she could have written, for they took far more

---

met some friends. When Garrett got up and said he was going to the bathroom, Dottie muttered: "He really has to use the telephone but he doesn't want to admit it."

24. Dottie: "An inch smaller and it would have been adultery. We had *Park-bench* for a cable address, but no one ever sent us one."

25. They considered having their door lettered UTICA DROP FORGE AND TOOL CO., ROBERT BENCHLEY, PRESIDENT—DOROTHY PARKER, PRESIDENT.

26. She put it quite succinctly in February 1928, in the guise of *The New Yorker's* "Constant Reader" looking for work: "Salary is no object; I want only enough to keep body and soul apart."

Five years earlier, in the June 1923 *Ainslee's,* she had calculated when she would be a millionaire: "I figure, by the way things are running now, I ought to have it piled up somewhere around the late spring of 2651."

time and effort than the verses and she lacked the discipline to do so. The quality of her poetry improved vastly with practice, and she became more proficient with the mechanics of the surprise or incongruous ending. It was soon her most characteristic touch. Readers learned to wait until the very last line of a stanza, or even of an entire piece, because it often contradicted all that preceded it. This device, perfected by Horace in the classical era, had recently become popular again, possibly through the critical success which attended the British writer H. H. Munro (Saki), who often employed it in the consummately polished short stories that he constructed during the first decade of the century. Munro had been killed during the last stages of the battle of the Somme in 1916, and his work was only just becoming familiar to refined American readers during the twenties.

But no matter how well she was received, Dorothy adamantly refused to take public pride in her work. In 1956 she declared that she only wrote "verses. I cannot say poems. Like everybody was then, I was following in the exquisite footsteps of Miss Millay, unhappily in my own horrible sneakers. Let's face it, honey, my verse is horribly dated—as anything once fashionable is dreadful now." But what was once "horribly dated" could again become fashionable, as happened after her death.

As her interest in Eddie waned, she spent increasing time with the other Algonks. Her close but probably platonic relationship with Benchley excited rumors that never quite disappeared, and Gertrude Benchley feared and despised her.[27] Dorothy liked

27. Many women thought that Dottie was particularly hard on her own sex, and hated and feared her for it. Much has been written about her purportedly celebrated feud with the editor and writer Clare Boothe Brokaw, later Luce. Dottie was even said to have mocked her name—"'Clare—Boothe—Luce'— sounds like the motto of a girl's school"—but it is almost certain that Dottie did not say the other things she was supposed to have said about her. So there is no reason to relate these two famous stories: First, that when they converged at a doorway, Clare smiled and stepped aside: "Age before beauty," and Dottie strolled through the door: "And pearls before swine." And second, at a dinner party, the actress Ilka Chase (the daughter of *Vogue* editor Edna Woolman

Neysa McMein, whose studio was across the hall from the Parkers' apartment. Neysa's was the usual Algonk late-afternoon haunt, and Dorothy happened by quite often, an easy enough chore when she could find Bernard Baruch or Herbert Bayard Swope conversing with Paul Robeson or Noël Coward while George Gershwin or Irving Berlin provided background music while Anaïs Nin posed for Neysa. Dorothy was a frequent visitor even after she moved to the Algonquin in October 1925.[28]

Aided by frequent references in The Conning Tower, Dorothy developed a formidable reputation for repartee at the Algonquin, at Neysa's, at Swope's palatial Manhattan apartment and even more opulent Great Neck estate (reputedly the model for Fitzgerald's Gatsby's),[29] at other country houses,[30] at dinners and

---

Chase) defended Clare by asserting that not only was Clare loyal to her friends, but "she's very kind to her inferiors." Dottie: "And where does she find them?"

28. She tortured the hotel manager Frank Case by seldom paying her rent on time and even telling him that he should feel lucky to have her staying there. Then a friend asked her if she was hanging up a stocking one Christmas. Dottie: "No, but I'm going to hang up Frank Case."

Once Case called her when he heard reports that she was breaking a house rule: "Do you have a gentleman in your room?" Dottie: "Just a minute. I'll ask him."

29. At one of Swope's Halloween parties, when Dottie asked why several people were standing around a washtub, she was told that "they're ducking for apples." Dottie: "There, but for a typographical error, is the story of my life." At another Swope party Dottie was talking with Maryland governor Albert Ritchie when someone at the table burped. There was a moment of strained silence, then . . . Dottie: "I'll get the Governor to pardon you."

30. Dottie found herself traveling to Long Island more than she professed to enjoy, as she complained in a 1927 *Life* piece: "No matter where I go, I always have to change at Jamaica."

In July 1925, she went with Frank Adams to the actress Fay Bainter's country house. Miss Bainter affectionately boasted that she and her husband had been married for seven years. Dottie: "Don't worry, he'll come back in style again."

When Aleck Woollcott and Dottie spent a bohemian weekend at Ruth Hale's dilapidated country house, they were aghast when they came upon an old battered toothbrush hanging from a nail over the basin, presumably there for communal use. Woollcott: "In God's name, what do you suppose [Ruth] does with that?" Dottie studied the thing for a moment: "I think she rides on it on Halloween."

parties,[31] playing games,[32] and just walking down the street.[33] But she was also secretly despised and feared by many people in her circle for what Edmund Wilson called her "treachery": she was notorious for taking pleasure in cordially talking to people one moment and then, as soon as their backs were turned, savaging them the next.[34]

Her drinking steadily increased, usually accompanied by Benchley or Heywood Broun. Before 1921 Benchley was the prig who warned Dorothy that drink would "coarsen" her, but he eventually took up the habit himself and soon became a compulsive alcoholic, adulterer, and spendthrift. They usually drank at speakeasies such as Tony Soma's[35] (Tony was the maternal grandfather of the actress Anjelica Huston) or Jack and Charlie's (later

31. The writer Charles MacArthur was wearing a white cotton suit, smoking a thin cigar, and holding a frosted glass when Dottie respectfully approached him at a summer party: "As the American consul here, sir——" She once dismissed a wealthy vulgarian as "a rhinestone in the rough."

32. Dottie excelled at the popular Algonquin game where the players challenged each other to use a long word in a punning sentence. She was challenged with "horticulture." Dottie: "You can lead a horticulture, but you can't make her think." She was challenged with "paroxysm." Dottie: "Paroxysm agnificent city." And in a 1927 book review: "I think I'm going to be able to use 'opium' in a sentence. I opium mother is feeling better. No, I guess I'm not, either."

Her musical variant: "Do you know the celery song: 'Celery gather at the river?' Or the Irish song, 'Irish I was in Dixie?' How about the French one? 'Je suis have no bananas?' Or the Spanish national anthem? 'Jose, can you see?' " And her question during a spirited game of Twenty Questions: "Would he be the kind of man who would put the wings back on flies?"

33. She hailed a taxi but the cabbie said: "I'm engaged." Dottie: "Then be happy."

34. Just after a woman left the room, Dottie started abusing her. A friend of the victim protested that the woman would not hurt a fly. Dottie: "Not if it was buttoned up."

On another occasion Dottie was particularly affable as she saw off a departing guest. Then: "That woman speaks eighteen languages, and can't say No in any of them."

35. Dorothy and Benchley were accosted there one night by another customer, who showed them a watch that he claimed was indestructible. The two friends promptly pounded the watch on the table, stamped on it, and then tested it some more. Finally the watch's owner grabbed it and put it to his ear: "It's stopped." They answered in unison: "Maybe you wound it too tight."

the restaurant "21"). Dorothy eventually decided that she preferred to drink Johnny Walker scotch whiskey neat, spacing her
sips so that she was seldom completely drunk, but seldom perfectly sober, either.[36] She would continue to drink vast amounts in
little sips for the rest of her life.

She met Charles MacArthur in 1922. He was two years
younger than she was; he was a charmer, a brawler, and a muscu-
lar and gifted journalist of the bare-knuckled Chicago school, a
world he would literally define six years later in the title of a play
he wrote with his old pal Ben Hecht, a smash Broadway hit called
The Front Page. Nearly everyone warned Dorothy that Charlie was
only interested in a good time—he was, ostensibly, married—but
she fell in love and started what would for the next decade
become a horrible pattern with several men: she beseeched, he
temporized; she whined, he withdrew; she accused, he cheated;
she sobbed, he left.

Dorothy's romantic disasters puzzled many observers. Many
men found her quite attractive, even after she started gaining
weight. Some, like the fastidious Edmund Wilson, were entranced
by her sexual allure but later professed to have been repelled by
her. She was tiny (various accounts put her height between four
feet eleven inches and five feet four inches) yet voluptuous, possessing fine features that were dominated by huge dark eyes and,
when she was so motivated, an often pleasant and even deferential
demeanor. Yet she was probably describing herself as well as the
flamboyant Isadora Duncan in a revealing 1928 *New Yorker* review:
"She had a knack for selecting the unworthy—perhaps all great
women have; one and all, they treated her with an extraordinary
shabbiness." If MacArthur did not treat her shabbily, he was at the
very least recklessly cavalier about the pain that she was suffering.

Dorothy found that she was pregnant and had an abortion, but

36. During the twenties, possibly at Tony Soma's, the bartender asked:
"What are you having?" Dottie: "Not much fun." Another time her good friend
John V. A. Weaver, the poet, dared to tell her that she was looking well. Dottie:
"Where the hell are you looking?"

MacArthur was unmoved.[37] Finally, deeply depressed and drinking heavily, she apparently attempted suicide by slashing her wrists with one of Eddie's old razors, but only after calling a local restaurant to deliver her dinner. The deliveryman found her and got her to the hospital.[38] Many of her friends thought she had done it to gain attention, and that is at least in part true. Over the next ten years she would appear to try to do away with herself at least three more times. First she swallowed an overdose of the sedative Veronal, but then she threw the glass out of the window at the last minute. Then she swallowed a bottle of shoe polish, which was messy but not lethal. Finally, she tried sleeping powders, but not enough to cause severe harm.[39]

After that first suicide attempt, Dorothy occasionally wore the scent of tuberose, which was traditionally used by undertakers on corpses. Her poetry also assumed a less breezy and topical tone. In March 1923, two months after that first suicide attempt, she published a poem titled "Triolet":

> *Give back the heart that I gave;*
>   *Keeping it never can mend it.*
> *See, I can smile, and be brave.*
> *Give back the heart that I gave,*
> *Hold it no more as your slave—*
>   *I've got a new place to send it.*
> *Give back the heart that I gave;*
>   *Keeping it never can mend it.*

37. The rumor mill buzzed with the story. Dottie: "It serves me right for putting all my eggs in one bastard." Another rumor had MacArthur putting up thirty dollars toward the abortion, which, according to Dottie, was like Judas making a refund.

38. At the hospital Dottie adorned her bandaged wrists with pale blue ribbons and then with black velvet ribbons and large bows: "I suppose you might as well know. I slashed my wrists. Eddie doesn't even have a sharp razor."

39. After that last attempt, in 1932, she recuperated at a woman friend's country estate, where she was so buffeted by attention that she fired off a despairing telegram to a possible rescuer: SEND ME A SAW INSIDE A LOAF OF BREAD.

Over the next ten years, there would be a depressing and star-tlingly lengthy succession of men sharing Dorothy's bed.[40] Marc Connelly described one of her beaus as "dandruff." Many of the trysts, including those with Deems Taylor, F. Scott Fitzgerald,[41] and possibly even Ring Lardner (his family was "skeptical" of the rumor) and Frank Adams, were transitory affairs. Other lovers, par-ticularly the gentle and generous pornography collector Seward Collins and the more virile Johns—Garrett and McClain—would last longer. Most would follow the MacArthur pattern, and none would work out.[42] As it happened, both MacArthur and McClain, two of the three men who broke her heart after leaving her, later moved in with her best friend, Robert Benchley.

A friend was later quoted as saying that Dorothy "was ignorant about money. All she knew was that she needed it." She often for-got to pay her taxes. She was a dreadful housekeeper and did not know how to cook. Someone said that she ate bacon raw because she did not know how to fry it. She spent whatever she made, usu-ally on scents, cigarettes, liquor, and clothes[43]—she loved hats—and was known to allow nearly anyone to come to the continuing

40. Reviewing a book of dating strategies in 1928, Dottie ruefully admitted that had she just played coquettish games, "maybe I could have been successful, instead of just successive."

41. Dottie met Fitzgerald through Edmund Wilson, who arranged a group lunch at the Algonquin. They were seated at a long and narrow table, one next to the other, with their backs to the wall. Dottie: "This looks like a road com-pany of the Last Supper."

In 1940, with his career in ashes, Fitzgerald died in Hollywood. At the funeral, Dottie looked at him in his coffin and repeated the famous line from the funeral of the title character of Fitzgerald's most noteworthy book, *The Great Gatsby:* "The poor son-of-a-bitch."

42. McClain was interested in wealthy women. At a cocktail party, Dottie shrugged after hearing him making a date with another woman. Dottie: "I have no squash courts. What can I do?" Then McClain left her for a rich Long Island hostess. Dottie: "He'll be back as soon as he has licked all the gilt off her ass." Her final verdict: "His body has gone to his head."

43. Dottie appeared to be shocked when she was told that an acquaintance was wearing a cape trimmed with monkey fur: "Really? I thought they were beards."

drinks party at her apartment so long as they brought a bottle with them.[44]

She had always aspired to be a genteel lady, a recognized poet, and a successful playwright. Despite her vaunted predatory instincts, she usually managed the first with surprising and even instinctive ease. The increasing quality of the work she was publishing in *Life, The Saturday Evening Post,* and, by early 1923, Frank Adams's Conning Tower column in *The World* lent increasing credibility to that second goal. For the third, in early 1924 she convinced the successful playwright Elmer Rice to collaborate with her on a project she had started. She also slept with him several times. She did not find the former Elmer Reizenstein attractive— he was Jewish, and looked it—but she managed to break off the affair without interfering with the play, which was called *Close Harmony.* They convinced the prominent Arthur Hopkins to produce it, but it still failed.[45] Perhaps the greatest mistake was to open on Broadway on December 1, the same night as Irving Berlin's newest *Music Box Revue* and the smash Adele and Fred Astaire hit *Lady Be Good.* Despite excellent reviews, *Close Harmony* grossed less than ten thousand dollars before closing after four weeks and only twenty-four performances. Dorothy was crushed. Her verdict: "It was dull. You have my apologies."[46]

44. Dottie: "All I need is room enough to lay a hat and a few friends." One time friends visited while she was bedridden with a cold. A very good but very drunk friend staggered in, emitting a succession of weird sounds as he struggled to speak. Dottie: "He thinks in French."

45. Dottie noticed that Hopkins was scrutinizing the actress Wanda Lyon's bouncing breasts during a dress rehearsal. Hopkins: "Dorothy, don't you think she ought to wear a brassiere in this scene?" Dottie: "God, no. You've got to have something in the show that moves." And when it became clear that the play was failing, she wired Robert Benchley: CLOSE HARMONY DID A COOL NINETY DOLLARS AT THE MATINEE. ASK THE BOYS IN THE BACK ROOM WHAT THEY WILL HAVE.

46. Dottie never lost her love for the theater and its characters. She particularly savored Tallulah Bankhead's sheer flamboyance, as when she inquired after Tallulah was particularly obstreperous at a party: "Has Whistler's Mother left yet?" Dottie visited the star's dressing room after an opening night performance: "Tallulah, your show is slipping."

Dottie once sent a congratulatory first-night telegram to the actress Uta

Meanwhile, Harold Ross had somehow inveigled the yeast heir Raoul Fleischmann to invest in his new cosmopolitan weekly magazine, which would be called The New Yorker. To pacify Fleischmann and others, Ross convinced Dorothy and several other well-known Algonquin friends to join a "board of editors" of the magazine.[47] She published "Cassandra Drops into Verse" in the magazine's second issue in February 1925, and over the remainder of the decade sold Ross more than fifty more poems and many prose pieces.

But in 1925, Dorothy was publishing most of her work without payment in Frank Adams's Conning Tower in The World.[48] On August 16, in the Sunday World, she printed "Some Beautiful Letters," six verses that included her two most famous pieces: "News Item" ("Men seldom make passes/At girls who wear glasses"), whose creation she forever lamented as "a terrible thing" for a person with serious literary ambitions; and the jauntily autobiographical "Résumé" (". . . Guns aren't lawful;/Nooses all give;/Gas smells awful;/You might as well live"), which was edited to its familiar form. Both were immediate sensations, but Dorothy's increasing fame spawned some petty artistic jealousy.

Adams had many other frequent contributors, including one

Hagen: A HAND ON YOUR OPENING AND MAY YOUR PARTS GROW BIGGER. But another time Dottie was goaded beyond endurance by an aging actress who had not worked in twenty years but still felt compelled to assure Dottie that "I just simply loathe the idea of leaving the theater, I'm so wedded to it." Dottie: "Why don't you sue, then, for non-support?"

47. The New Yorker only survived during its early desperate years through ruthless economy. During that first summer of 1925 Ross found Dottie in a speakeasy and demanded to know why she was not at work turning out quotable things. Dottie: "Someone was using the pencil."

48. The humorist Frank Sullivan took over The Conning Tower when Frank Adams left on a two-month honeymoon in May 1925. More than forty years later, just after Dottie died, Sullivan recalled that he "had a hell of a time filling that column. Dotty heard about it at Swope's or Tony Soma's or somewhere, or with her intuition sensed it from reading my flounderings, and by God one day two poems arrived from her! I still remember the note she sent with them: 'If you can't use these, give them to some poor family.'" She later sent Sullivan two more poems.

Elspeth MacDuffie O'Halloran (pen name "Elspeth"), whose work was similar, but vastly inferior, to Dorothy's. Adams reported in his November 17, 1926, Diary entry that "unless somebody should be John Milton in a few days" he was going to give that year's coveted watch to Dorothy for "The Dark Girl's Rhyme."[49] Adams's announcement was evidently more than Elspeth could bear, because she soon submitted a challenge "To Dorothy Parker." After declaring her own literary burden in stanza one, and whining that Dorothy was columnist's pet in stanza two, Elspeth got to the point—Adams's watch prediction—in stanza three:

> *Of course, I'm glad it's Dorothy.*
> *I'm thrilling with delight.*
> *But how I'd like to meet that girl*
> *Alone some ebon night!*

It ran on November 23. Dorothy was drinking very heavily and was deeply depressed at the time. She had recently made her second suicide attempt (Veronal) and was seeing a psychiatrist,[50] but she responded "To Elspeth" in The Conning Tower the very next day:

> *Lady, I have read your verse on*
> *Me—the one wherein you write*
> *"How I'd like to meet that person*
> *All alone some ebon night!"*

49. Also in the Diary entry for the same date, Adams related that "Dorothy Parker came to see me, and I overjoyed to see her, and she told me about her peregrinations abroad, and I asked her about Ernest Hemingway, and how old he was, and she said, 'Well, I don't know. You know, all writers are either twenty-nine or Thomas Hardy.'" Hardy was eighty-six at the time.

50. She soon stopped seeing the psychiatrist, Alvan Barach, because "I've never seen a cure." Her good friend, the noted pianist and wit Oscar Levant, later also saw Barach. Once Levant asked Dottie if she took sleeping pills. Yes, she replied, "in a big bowl with sugar and cream."

Levant later shuttled in and out of psychiatric hospitals, including one that served dinner at 4:45 P.M. Dottie: "That makes for a nice long evening." Dottie on Levant: "He long ago said everything about everything—and what Oscar Levant has said, *stays* said."

Though your wish to wound were little,
You have done your worst—you see,
Some one, when my heart was brittle,
Said those very words to me.

Lady, take my humble greetings;
Take my thanks; but let me say
Were it not for midnight meetings,
I'd be on my feet to-day.

A friend once said of her that "Dottie can only do her best work when her heart is breaking" and, at the time of the Elspeth scrap, Dorothy was preparing to release the first book of her collected verse. Though she was convinced that her work was "not good enough" to be published in book form, Horace Liveright of the publishing house Boni and Liveright had already commissioned a similar project with another popular writer of light verse, Samuel Hoffenstein, and was confident that her collection would succeed. In early 1926 he broached the subject. Dorothy considered it and, when she realized that the book could supply the money she would need if she wanted to take an extended trip to Europe, she agreed.

She felt that very little of her early work was good enough to appear in the book. While most of it was considerably less polished than her more recent experiments, in retrospect it is also clear that she deliberately chose to include those verses whose substance and style reflected what she hoped to project as her own, that is, the scarred and astringent modern woman, spare and unadorned, making her way through a new and starkly modern world, experienced in sex but cynical of love, defying all comers with a quip and a sneer—or a private sigh. Dorothy Parker usually felt most confident of her artistic abilities when she was writing about Dorothy Parker.

Dorothy ruthlessly discarded those "cute" pieces and the hate verses that did not fit the aesthetic profile she hoped to project.

But after rejecting most of her previous work, Dorothy desperately needed more verses, so while she was in Europe she briskly wrote nearly forty more, including the raggedly exuberant "Song of Americans Resident in France."[51] More than thirty of these ended up in the book.

Enough Rope was released in December 1926. It was both a popular and a personal triumph, for it established, as *The World's* reviewer put it, Dorothy's "secure position as one of the most sparkling wits who express themselves through light verse," with "the higher plane of authentic poetry . . . within her reach." The line that divides light verse and serious "authentic" poetry is an obscure one, and the distinction often hinges more on the pomposity of the judge than on the merits of the work. The road between Nantucket and Xanadu is littered with hopeful submissions. Added *The New York Times:* "Miss Parker's is not society verse in the old sense; it is flapper verse. And as such it is wholesome, engaging, uncorseted and not devoid of grace."

The influence of the book, and its effect on Dorothy's reputation, eventually led to some historical revisionism. While the book did sell forty-seven thousand copies, which was an impressive showing for a volume of poetry, that level of popularity was by no means as unique as was later assumed. The leading novelists of the time, such as Sinclair Lewis[52] and Edna Ferber,[53] often sold in the hundreds of thousands, and even Samuel Hoffenstein, that

51. In Paris, Dottie often saw but never met the famously reserved James Joyce: "I guess he's afraid he might drop a pearl." The Monte Carlo casino refused to admit her until she was properly dressed: "So I went and found my stockings, and then came back and lost my shirt." Returning home, the transatlantic crossing was "so rough that the only thing I could keep on my stomach was the first mate."

52. In a New York nightclub a few years later, Dottie overheard the conversation of the next table, a group of visiting midwestern governors: "Sounds like overwritten Sinclair Lewis."

53. Dottie was jealous of Ferber's professional fluidity: "I understand Ferber whistles at her typewriter. And there was that poor sucker Flaubert rolling around on his floor for three days looking for the right words." Because Dottie agonized over every word in her own work, she damned those prolific authors

other poet signed by Horace Liveright, sold sixty-three thousand copies of his first collection, *Poems in Praise of Practically Nothing*. Yet Samuel Hoffenstein slipped into permanent obscurity, and Dorothy's idol, Edna St. Vincent Millay, is infrequently read, but Dorothy Parker is still the subject of fascination.[54] Dorothy's perspective and expression have somehow resonated through an influential slice of the literary public for more than seventy years and continue to do so in the present. Perhaps it is the iconoclasm or the calculated irreverence, or perhaps the gaunt and distinctly contemporary candor, but there is something there, particularly in her verses, that draws an audience far beyond what the polite but dismissive reviewers could have dreamed.

During the following years she released two more collections of her verses, *Sunset Gun* in 1928 and *Death and Taxes* in 1931, which sold succeedingly fewer copies. Viking Press later compiled the verses from the first three books and, after Dorothy deleted yet another fifteen that she no longer wanted remembered and added five more that she had written in the intervening years, issued *Not So Deep as a Well* in 1936.[55] She also published two collections of short fiction, *Laments for the Living,* which received generally positive reviews, in 1930, and *After Such Pleasures* in 1933. Viking also issued a compilation of the fiction in 1939, with a few new pieces, under the title *Here Lies.* The best of the short stories was "Big Blonde," which was published in Seward Collins's *The Bookman* in February 1929. It later won the coveted O. Henry competition (and five hundred dollars) for the best short story of that year.

Since October 1927, Dorothy had also gained notice as *The New Yorker*'s book reviewer, "Constant Reader." Though she possessed

---

who benefited from America's "proud confusion" of industry and talent: "It is our national joy to mistake for the first-rate, the fecund rate."

54. Dottie: "Yeah, that's me, the toast of two continents—Greenland and Australia."

55. She dedicated it to Frank Adams, the erudite Comma Hunter of Park Row, who, she once declared, "raised me from a couplet."

formidable critical skills and refined tastes, she again found that she often preferred abuse to edification.[56] She also assumed Robert Benchley's drama chores after he went to Hollywood, with similar results.[57] She had trouble meeting deadlines,[58] and though the reviews were very popular, they only appeared intermittently

56. Dottie later admitted that "it's easier to write about those you hate—just as it's easier to criticize a bad play or a bad book." Some of her most famous cracks appeared in her *New Yorker* column and, a quarter-century later, a few more in her vastly more mellow *Esquire* book reviews. She is invariably credited with "This is not a novel to be tossed aside lightly. It should be thrown with great force" and "It was written without fear and without research," and her observation that one author was "a writer for the ages—for the ages four to eight." But there were many others:

The President's Daughter: Revealing the Love-Secret of President Harding (addressing alleged police attempts to confiscate the printer's plates): "Lady, . . . those weren't policemen; they were critics of literature dressed up."

Lay Sermons, by the author of *The Autobiography of Margot Asquith* "(four volumes, neatly boxed, suitable for throwing purposes)": "The affair between Margot Asquith and Margot Asquith will live as one of the prettiest love stories in all literature." "This book of essays . . . has all the depth and glitter of a worn dime."

Crude: "It is also a criticism of it." *Shoot If You Must:* "This must be a gift book. That is to say, a book which you wouldn't take on any other terms." *Mistress of Mellyn:* "It is derived from Jane Eyre as painstakingly as a fingerprint is taken from the butt of a gun." *A Matter of Life and Death:* She could not "see eye-to-eye with the one who hailed the book as 'Literature with a capital L.' . . . 'Length with a capital L' is more like it."

Dottie particularly loathed A. A. Milne's "Pooh" books and the cutesy language he affected (a year earlier she had written a nasty verse, "When We Were Very Sore," upon learning that she had been advertised as "America's A. A. Milne," which, in turn, had caused Robert Benchley to call her "Dottie-the-Pooh"): "And it is that word 'hummy,' my darlings, that marks the first place in *The House at Pooh Corner* at which Tonstant Weader fwowed up."

57. For example, on Channing Pollack's 1931 play: "*The House Beautiful* is for me the play lousy." Contrary to common belief, she never reviewed *The Lake*, though she may have quipped that Katharine Hepburn "ran the whole gamut of emotion from A to B" as an offhand remark during intermission. She also pretended not to have heard of the star of *The Respectful Prostitute:* "Meg Mundy? What's that, a Welsh holiday?"

58. When *The New Yorker* pressed for overdue reviews, she was "too fucking busy and vice versa." Her overriding philosophy was, "Work is the province of cattle."

between 1928 and 1933, when Constant Reader permanently hung up her bookmark.

But Dorothy was sinking deeper into her personal quagmire. She started a novel, collected an advance, and never finished it. She had little money and borrowed constantly from carefully selected friends;[59] she was drinking heavily at the nearly nightly cocktail parties she both threw and attended,[60] which caused her to run to alcoholic fat and, on occasion, black out; she also continued to get involved in hopeless love affairs.[61] She tried to escape her problems by moving, first to the Hotel Lowell on the East Side

59. In January 1931, Constant Reader observed that "when your bank account is so overdrawn that it is positively photographic, steps must be taken." Dottie claimed she dreamed of a rural life "raising cheques."

In December 1932, the *New York Herald Tribune* asked her for a list of the ten most beautiful words in the English language. Dottie: "To me the most beautiful word in the English language is cellar-door. Isn't it wonderful? The ones I like, though, are 'cheque' and 'inclosed.'"

60. Dottie's drinking caused even Benchley to suggest that she consider Alcoholics Anonymous. After one meeting, she met him at Tony's. Benchley: "Are you going to join?" Dottie: "Certainly not. They want me to stop *now*."

There were many parties, usually involving alcohol, and there were many victims. Dottie professed to despise some party-goers because "their pooled emotions wouldn't fill a teaspoon." She was cornered at one party by a pretentious young man, the sort she once referred to as "a pony's ass," who subjected her to his brilliance at some length, concluding with: "I simply can't bear fools." Dottie: "How odd. Apparently your mother could." At another party, she came across an actor, presumably American, whose season on the London stage had caused him to affect British pronunciation as he repeatedly referred to his "shedule." Dottie: "If you don't mind my saying so, I think you're full of skit." And at another party, their domineering hostess was described as "outspoken." Dottie: "By whom?" At another, she was asked if she had enjoyed herself. Dottie: "Enjoyed it? One more drink and I'd have been under the host."

It got so that other party-goers eagerly waited for her remarks. One young man actually followed her around hoping she would say something before he finally admitted: "You're not at all the way I thought you'd be. I'm sorry." Dottie: "That's all right. But do me a favor. When you get home, throw your mother a bone." And, finally, at another party a woman approached her: "Are you Dorothy Parker?" Dottie: "Yes, do you mind?"

61. In March 1933 she wrote of times "when one had put sex carefully away on the highest cupboard-shelf, in a box marked 'Winter Hats—1916.'"

and then to a nearby apartment;[62] and also by traveling, to Hollywood and an MGM studio job for a few unhappy months in
1928,[63] and to Europe four times between 1926 and 1932.[64] She
was particularly depressed and lonely during one European trip,
and sent a desperate and entreating letter to an old beau in New
York. He replied by telegram—collect: LOVED LETTER DEAR SO
HAPPY YOU ARE WELL.

During the spring of 1933,[65] Benchley introduced Dorothy to
Alan Campbell, a delicately handsome[66] actor and writer who was
eleven years younger than she was. Alan was from Richmond, Vir-
ginia, of Scotch and Jewish ancestry (in his case, it was the
mother[67] who was Jewish), whose looks, most happily for
Dorothy, took after his father's side. Though Dorothy was sensitive

62. The latter apartment overlooked the East River: "far enough east to
plant tea." In a 1928 book review Dottie claimed she wanted to live at "Rising
Gorge." Some years earlier she had come up with "Wit's End," which Aleck
Woollcott used for his own East Side apartment.

63. On Christmas Day 1928, Frank Adams reported that Dottie tried to
relieve her loneliness in her own way: "When the [studio] sign painter arrived
to put her name on the door, she bribed him to leave it off and substitute
instead the simple legend: 'GENTLEMEN.' "

64. On one occasion, running late as usual, Dottie was shoved on board her
departing liner by George Oppenheimer and others. Soon she appeared at the
rail: "Guess who's on the boat—Marlene Dietrich! And guess who's not on the
boat—my trunk!" Her passage was probably paid by Cross leather goods heirs
Sara and Gerald Murphy, who were living in the Swiss Alps while their tuber-
cular son was undergoing treatment. Dottie spent much of her trip as their
guest, and she bought a lamb coat with "all the warmth and durability of a sheet
of toilet paper" in order to battle the elements. She sent Frank Adams a postcard: "Sleeping under avalanches. Wish you were with us."

65. Earlier that year, Benchley told her that former president Calvin
Coolidge was dead. Dottie: "How can they tell?"

66. They were drinking at Tony Soma's when Campbell suddenly got up and
stalked off. Dottie: "I don't know why he should get so angry, just because I
called him a fawn's ass."

67. Dottie's soon-to-be mother-in-law, Hortense Campbell, was a harri-
dan. Some years after the marriage, Dottie and Lillian Hellman were content-
edly knitting in front of a roaring fire in the living room while Alan and Horte
conducted a noisy argument upstairs. Finally Alan stormed down the stairs:
"It's as hot as hell in here." Dottie: "Not for orphans."

about the age difference,[68] and there was some talk that Alan had engaged in some sort of homosexual activity,[69] they soon settled into a comfortable routine. Alan was charming and considerate, and he possessed many of the traits that Dorothy sorely lacked, including frugality, neatness, discipline, and organization. He was also only a pedestrian writer, and he greatly admired Dorothy's vastly superior talents and reputation. They married in June.[70]

In August 1934 they signed ten-week contracts to write screenplays for Paramount Pictures in Hollywood, at two hundred fifty dollars per week for Alan and one thousand dollars per week for Dorothy. Alan's contract also called for him to act. For several years they earned two thousand dollars a week—for a short time, more than five thousand dollars—and if they claimed to despise both the town[71] and its products,[72] they were, for a

68. Dottie: "I'm thinking of sending him to military school when he's old enough."

69. Dottie's view of homosexuality mirrored the attitudes of her time. She dined in Paris with some lesbians who asked her opinion of same-sex marriage. Dottie: "Of course you must have legal marriages. The children have to be considered." Back at a bar in Greenwich Village a few years later, Dottie and Alan Campbell were accosted by a customer who appeared flamboyantly gay and who asked if she read fairy tales. Dottie: "My dear, let's not talk shop."

As to a notoriously homosexual English actor: "He simply buggers description." And: "Scratch an actor and find an actress."

When Dottie prepared to leave Los Angeles for the final time in 1964, an effete realtor who lived nearby found some people who were interested in her house. While the prospects looked the place over, the neighbor sat with Dottie and basked in her compliments. Finally he got up to check on his customers. Dottie: "There he goes, tossing his little Shirley Temple curls."

70. Dottie was very jealous of other women. When Alan performed in a play, she said the female lead looked like "a two-dollar whore who once commanded five."

71. Dottie praised Budd Schulberg's 1941 vitriolic novel about Hollywood, *What Makes Sammy Run?*: "I never thought anyone could put Hollywood—the true shittiness of the place—between covers." She once said of a producer: "He hasn't got sense enough to bore assholes in wooden hobbyhorses."

Once Alan found her examining a photograph in a local newspaper. There were three elephants in the picture: one in a silk hat, another in a clerical collar, and the third in a bridal veil. Dottie: "I give it six months." And she turned the page.

72. She wired season's greetings to the writer Joe Bryan: IN ORDER TO

while at least, one of its most popular couples.[73] Yet they left Hollywood with neither fortune[74] nor reputation enhanced.

It is not that the films they wrote were badly received or lost money, but they were generally undistinguished. Though Alan had good work habits and a solid sense of structure, and Dorothy was often superb with dialogue, the result was usually lackluster. The studio moguls may have possessed banal tastes, but they knew how to produce popular, well-made movies, and they certainly knew who their top talents were. The top rank of the writers A-list could include a former Algonk such as Donald Ogden Stewart, or a peripheral Round Tabler such as Ben Hecht, but not Dorothy Parker and Alan Campbell.

The common perception was that Alan was the classic Hollywood husband who only worked because he was married to the talented wife, but in fact he might actually have been the better screenwriter of the two and, with his vastly superior work habits, probably the more valuable property. Budd Schulberg, a noted

---

WISH YOU A MERRY CHRISTMAS I AM INTERRUPTING WORK ON MY SCREEN EPIC, LASSIE GET DOWN.

73. Once Dottie saw the writer Louis Adamic at a summer dinner party wearing a rumpled white cotton suit: "Looks like he's come to sell us some leaf tobacco!"

When Dottie moved to Hollywood in the mid thirties, most of the metropolitan area was still undeveloped. Once she and Aleck Woollcott visited someone who lived on the edge of the wilderness. Their host took them outside to watch wild animals come for the plate of food that was left there. The animals did not appear. They were urged to return, and again they waited, this time until eleven-thirty, without luck. Their host was dejected: "Oh, I don't understand it. How could it happen?" Dottie: "I thought we'd at *least* get the after-theater crowd."

74. Dottie: "Hollywood money isn't money. It's congealed snow, melts in your hand." The journalist Vincent Sheean once came to visit, and they got into a joking discussion of burial arrangements. Dottie: "I want to be buried in a shroud made of unpaid bills from Valentina."

The writer Kyle Crichton once came across Dottie at a grocery store and asked how she liked Hollywood. Dottie: "Oh, it's all right. You make a little money and get caught up on your debts. We're up to 1912 now." Yet when a producer asked her to write a script, Dottie was offended by his offer: "You can't take it with you, and even if you did, it would probably melt."

screenwriter and novelist who was closely involved in the events of that time, believed that Dorothy could not have held a job without Alan. When their marriage started to go sour, Dorothy tried to prove to Alan that he was expendable by getting herself fired from *The Pride of the Yankees*. She waited for Sam Goldwyn to get rid of Alan, but Goldwyn kept Alan on and hired a new writer to replace Dorothy.

The producers may have tended to expect more from Dorothy because they assumed that she was the artist but, as the playwright Tom Stoppard observed more than thirty years later, "skill without imagination is craftsmanship," and Dorothy, who never possessed that extraordinary creative spark, was only a diligent craftsman. She owed her literary success to a combination of craft, wit, calculated irreverence, and observation—but not artistic vision. She knew how the language worked and how to put words together, and for all the reports of her fabled indolence, in truth she strained to make every single thing she wrote as good as she was capable of doing. "I can't write five words but that I change seven," she once confessed. But writing plays and movies required the imagination to *create* compelling characters and absorbing stories, and that was a quality she lacked. She needed ideas, not craft, and she failed.

During their years in Hollywood, Dorothy and Alan worked for some of the finest producers in the industry, including Sam Goldwyn[75] and David Selznick, and for a time at the most prestigious studio, Metro-Goldwyn-Mayer.[76] The pinnacle of their screenwriting career was the Academy Award nomination they received for *A Star Is Born* in 1937, although it is impossible to

75. The following line has been attributed to Dottie and several others. In a story conference, Goldwyn, who had once been a glove maker, scolded someone, who retorted: "Don't you point that finger at me. I knew it when it had a thimble on it!"

But it was Dottie who responded to Goldwyn's demand that her screenplay end on a happy note: "I know this will come as a shock to you, Mr. Goldwyn, but in all history, which has held billions and billions of human beings, not a single one ever had a happy ending."

76. Dottie had her own version: "Metro-Goldwyn-Merde."

determine just how much of that film, or any film, they actually wrote, because the studio system of the thirties and forties often assigned a dozen or more writers to any given script. Dorothy later claimed that she neither contributed much to the screenplay nor ever saw the completed picture from beginning to end, but she was notoriously and often deliberately inaccurate about such things. Dorothy and Alan also contributed to the classic *Nothing Sacred,* which was released the same year, and Dorothy worked on Alfred Hitchcock's *Saboteur* four years later (she and Hitchcock appeared together in the film as a couple driving down a highway), but they spent most of their time on forgettable comedies, musicals, and light dramas. They ultimately accumulated more than fifteen screenwriting credits.[77]

77. She also wrote some verse in Hollywood. She met Somerset Maugham at a Fanny Brice dinner party, and Maugham challenged her to write him a poem on the spot. She blithely agreed and started with a familiar nursery rhyme:

Higgledy Piggledy, my white hen;
She lays eggs for gentlemen.

Dottie once said that she felt uncomfortable around Englishmen of a certain class—"whenever I meet one of these Britishers I feel as if I have a papoose on my back"—but on this occasion she was evidently quite at ease, for when Maugham admitted that the lines had long been favorites of his, Dottie completed her rhyme:

You cannot persuade her with gun or lariat
To come across for the proletariat.

But she denied writing the verse in William Randolph Hearst's San Simeon guest book:

Upon my honor
I saw a Madonna
Standing in a niche
Above the door
Of a prominent whore
Of a prominent son of a bitch.

It referred to Hearst and his mistress, the actress Marion Davies. Though the verse was quite popular, Dottie was livid that anyone thought she would rhyme *honor* and *Madonna.*

Dorothy had exhibited little interest in either politics[78] or social issues before she joined much of the rest of the world in watching the dramatic final appeals of Nicola Sacco and Bartolomeo Vanzetti in 1927. The self-described anarchists had been condemned for two murders near Boston seven years before. For some reason the fate of the two immigrant radicals affected her and she jumped into the fray, along with her fellow Algonks Robert Benchley, Heywood Broun, and Ruth Hale. Perhaps her sudden and intense commitment was due to Gardner "Pat" Jackson, a handsome communist fellow traveler of the familiar physical type. Jackson ran the clemency campaign's Boston office, and that is where Dorothy volunteered to work. Before the anarchists were executed, Dorothy and Ruth Hale were detained by the Boston police in one of the first gentle celebrity political arrests. They were not even fingerprinted[79] before they were released; Dorothy pleaded guilty and was fined five dollars for loitering and sauntering.

Over the ensuing decade Dorothy was imperfectly yet increasingly radicalized, but if her conversation was occasionally infected with the hoary vocabulary of socialist platitudes, and if she attended a succession of dreary meetings, her normal life continued on its usual path. During the thirties, as the worst sufferings caused by the Great Depression affected great swaths of society, there were new issues and campaigns. In early 1933, Adolf Hitler assumed power in Germany and enacted a horrifying sequence of anti-Semitic legislation. Though Dorothy had never before shown any particular interest in her Jewish background, Hitler

78. Dottie had even warned Heywood Broun against working at the radical and intellectually pretentious *Nation* magazine during the mid twenties: "You won't be able to hear a thing for the clanking of Phi Beta Kappa keys."

She had already dismissed the fastidiously overrefined tastes of the readers of the other main organ of the left, an affectation evidently epitomized by its editor, Herbert David Croly: "They have a conscious exquisiteness, a deep appreciation of their own culture. They exude an atmosphere of the *New Republic*—a sort of Crolier-than-thou air."

79. Though Dottie charged at the time that "they left me a few of theirs. The big stiffs!"

terrified her. By the spring of 1936 she and Donald Ogden Stewart were hosting a one-hundred-dollars-a-plate dinner to raise money for what was called the Hollywood Anti-Nazi League.

Stewart was an interesting case. He had been a light satirist and humorist who had been even less interested in politics than Dorothy, and who had sneered at her interest in Sacco and Vanzetti. Yet, for some reason, he became radicalized after he moved to Hollywood and achieved great professional success and remuneration. Stewart was quickly divorced by his socialite wife, Beatrice (one of Dorothy's closest friends), who despised his new politics, and he became enamored with and ultimately married Ella Winter, the attractive Australian-born widow of the muckraker Lincoln Steffens. There is a substantial amount of information now emerging from the former Soviet archives, some of which indicates that Ella had been, according to one former apparatchik, "one of the most trusted party agents for the West Coast" for several years. She was assigned to infiltrate and help radicalize Hollywood, and to target people such as Stewart, as she had done with Steffens. Stewart was pleasant and sincere, but he was also a political naïf who was putty in Ella's hands.

In later years, when the Soviet Union was allied with the United States in the Second World War, members of the Hollywood Anti-Nazi League were still condemned for being "premature Anti-Fascists." It was, in reality, a Soviet front organization. The speaker at that 1936 dinner was Otto Katz, a communist propagandist working under an imaginative Stalinist functionary called Willi Münzenburg with orders to build communist influence in the center of world popular culture. Stalin hoped to sway the democracies through the mass media, chiefly by picking at the inadequacies of the capitalist system and its policies. The Depression and its attendant social miseries was one promising avenue. The plight of the Scottsboro Boys, and the larger issue of racial injustice, was another. The rise of Hitler was a third. The Spanish Civil War, which was, in essence, a battle between surrogates of Hitler and Stalin, was a fourth. Closer to home, the battle to establish an independent writer's union in Hollywood was a fifth.[80]

Though the far left's position on most of these issues was defensible, and even admirable, it also insisted that there was only the single doctrinaire stance on each; it maintained that isolated and often transitory problems were invariably "symptoms" of a diseased whole, and that any attempt to explore or discuss the vastly greater moral dilemmas that were emerging in the Soviet Union, or to compare them with conditions in the democracies, was inherently "fascist."

Katz wanted to recruit people such as Stewart and Dorothy, celebrated artists leading extravagantly luxurious and glamorous lives who wondered whether there was something wrong with that. Ian Hamilton, the author of *Writers in Hollywood, 1915–1951,* noted that they were

> thought of in Hollywood, and elsewhere, as the dandy converts, the pixie revolutionists: New York wisecrackers lured to Hollywood by the big money and now self-politicized in order to assuage their guilt: guilt about writing for films and earning mammoth salaries at the height of the Depression, guilt about having had such a good time during the twenties . . . impressionable and often guilty.

The byzantine corridors of leftist American thought during the thirties were a rat's nest that defies any concise explication. There were, however, three distinct major strains. On its right were the mainstream New Deal liberals, who usually supported Franklin D. Roosevelt and most of the existing economic and social order, but who believed that some reforms were essential for it to survive. This group included Robert Benchley and most

80. A screenwriter dared to tell her that he did not think creative writers belong in unions. Dottie: "That sonofabitch telling me that *he's* a creative writer? If he's a creative writer, I'm Marie of Rumania!" Dottie even delivered a speech to some cartoonists: "Now, look, baby, 'union' is spelled with *five* letters. It is *not* a four-letter word."

of the literary class. To their left were the democratic socialists, who supported parts of the present system and were basically patriotic, but who also suspected the profit motive and what they saw as the untrammeled power of the plutocrats. This group included Heywood Broun and most of the rest of the literati.

On the far left were the embattled Trotskyites, who followed the deposed Leon Trotsky, and the Stalinists, usually so described by their opponents. The Stalinists presumed to support various high-minded policies that promised to lead to the socialist utopia of equality, prosperity, and peace, but, as Edmund Wilson put it in a May 1944 *New Yorker* review, Dorothy

> succumbed to the expiatory mania that has become epidemic with film writers and was presently making earnest appeals on behalf of those organizations which talked about being "progressive" and succeeded in convincing their followers that they were working for social revolution, though they had really no other purpose than to promote the foreign policy of Stalin.

Dorothy not only backed the left's correct position on the "easy" issues, and even dressed the part by affecting the dowdy proletarian dirndled peasant look around chic Hollywood, but she also slavishly followed the vastly less popular Stalinist line on the two key litmus tests that arose later in the decade. She signed a petition that endorsed the verdicts that were handed down from the notorious show trials that accompanied the Great Purge of 1936–38, during which Stalin put millions of his own people to death. The murderous rampage caused most previously loyal communists and fellow travelers to denounce Stalin and move to the right, but not Dorothy.

And then, in August 1939, Stalin signed the infamous non-aggression pact with Hitler, which caused virtually all of the remaining independent hard left to publicly abandon Stalin. But when the leaders of the Hollywood Anti-Nazi League, including

Dorothy, heard of the agreement, they leaped into action—and immediately changed the name of their organization to the Hollywood League for Democratic Action, presumably on orders to avoid offending their new allies. Some of Dorothy's supporters have claimed that she was shocked and appalled by the pact, but there is no contemporaneous evidence to sustain that sublimely convenient assertion. In fact, she doggedly refused to issue any public criticism of it, even though she had been moved to radicalism partly because of the West's lukewarm response to Hitler's Jew-baiting policies.

While it is not certain whether Dorothy formally joined the Communist party, she probably did. She publicly declared herself to be a communist in 1934 (though there was a tinge of adolescent grandiosity to the statement), and she invoked the Fifth Amendment when she was specifically asked twenty years later. But it is clear that despite her emotional sentimentality, her intellectual incoherence, and the utter lack of discipline that characterized, inter alia, her flirtation with the revolutionary struggle, she was by any reasonable definition a Stalinist. Stephen Koch, who has written extensively on the subject, observed that "Parker's union of style and Stalinist attitudes was a natural fit. Through the chic of her hard-left commitments, Parker could both validate her love of glamour, and mask it with an appropriate look of disdain for all the vanities." And according to Bea Stewart, Dorothy "was not a personal friend of the multitudes. She was a very, very *grande dame,* and contrariness was the wellspring of her communism. She was anti. She was anti the Establishment."

If communism helped humanity, then she was, in her own simplistic, romantic way, a communist, and dialectic be damned. Some apologists later excused her actions because she meant well, a useful defense that is routinely employed by erstwhile radicals, but seldom afforded to even the most repentant former reactionaries. But even if Dorothy's intent *was* pure, which is doubtful, she still condoned, and outspokenly supported, and even helped finance the monstrous policies of a hostile and genocidal regime. Determining whether she was a rogue or merely a fool is a melancholy task.

Dorothy's excursion through the hard left cost her many friendships,[81] most notably Robert Benchley's, and her viciously ad hominem intolerance for opposing views caused her to cut loose from most of her remaining longstanding relationships, including those with Bea Stewart and Sara and Gerald Murphy. It ultimately put her name near the top of some of the blacklists that circulated through the industry[82] and effectively destroyed what remained of her screenwriting career, but she never wavered and even attracted a new confidante, with Svengalian overtones, along the way.

Lillian Hellman was a gifted playwright and a doctrinaire Stalinist (though she also would have bridled at the label) who was twelve years younger than Dorothy. They became close friends in the mid thirties, shortly after Hellman broke into the popular consciousness before her thirtieth birthday with the remarkable success (nearly seven hundred Broadway performances) of her first produced play, *The Children's Hour*. Perhaps it was Hellman's success at such a young age, in a field that Dorothy so dearly wished to conquer herself, that led Dorothy to ascribe some greater insight or comprehension to her than Hellman in fact deserved. Whatever the reason, Hellman quickly gained, and jealously guarded, an intellectual and emotional ascendency over Dorothy that endured through the final thirty years of Dorothy's life.

Dorothy greatly admired Hellman's lover, the writer Dashiell Hammett, though Hammett intensely disliked Dorothy and avoided her whenever possible. Hammett was even more radical than Hellman: for example, during the 1940 Battle of Britain,

81. She tended to hector, as when advising a presumably astigmatic political moderate: "Stop looking at the world through rose-colored bifocals."

82. While she was blacklisted in the late forties, a drunk harassed her at a bar. Dottie: "With the crown of thorns I wear, why should I be bothered with a prick like you?"

when that country was fighting for its life against German bombers, but a year before Hitler negated the 1939 nonaggression pact by attacking the Soviet Union, Hammett was a leader of a Stalinist Hollywood front organization whose sole aim was to gratuitously dash British hopes of American aid. It was called, with the instinctive vulgarity of the True Believer Thug, "The-Yanks-Are-Not-Coming Committee." It was probably Hellman, with surreptitious help from Hammett, who molded Dorothy's increasingly extreme politics during the late thirties and helped maintain it through the forties.

Meanwhile, the poetry compilation *Not So Deep as a Well* went through five printings and comprised the greater part of the more than thirty thousand dollars in royalties that Dorothy earned between 1935 and 1937. But the Campbells, and particularly Dorothy, often spent more than they made, and in 1936 they splurged on the Fox House, a colonial farmhouse and barn on more than one hundred acres in scenic Bucks County, Pennsylvania, north of Philadelphia. They paid a bargain price of less than five thousand dollars for it, but then spent ninety-eight thousand dollars to renovate and landscape the property.[83] They shuttled between Hollywood and Bucks County until Alan enlisted in the Army Air Corps in 1942, and they eventually sold the farm in 1947—for forty thousand dollars.[84]

They sold it because they were getting divorced. The first years of the marriage were happy enough, and Dorothy was uncharacteristically civil to her new husband until she suffered miscarriages, first in 1936 and again in 1939,[85] the latter soon followed

83. Several other writers who lived nearby were incensed when Dottie and Alan cut down some trees on the property. Dottie: "Fifty-second Street Thoreaus."

84. The columnist Leonard Lyons asked her to describe the property in two words. Dottie: "Want it?"

85. There was some worry about her lack of maternal instincts. Thomas Guinzburg, the son of the cofounder of the Viking Press, was a child at the time, and he once overheard Dottie: "Oh, my, if only the Guinzburg children were as well behaved as the Guinzburg dogs."

She was fascinated by Joe Bryan's six-year-old son, John, and his ability to

by a hysterectomy. Some psychological alchemy caused Dorothy to release her anger by viciously turning on Alan. She gained a lot of weight—Gertrude Benchley claimed Dorothy considered having a breast-reduction operation in the late thirties—and increased her drinking even further, causing Alan to also drink excessively to keep up with her. She took pleasure in publicly humiliating him, especially by accusing him of a fondness for young men, just as nearly twenty years before she had publicly accused Eddie Parker of drug addiction. After Pearl Harbor she insisted that Alan enlist and was inordinately pleased when he enrolled as a private, as one of the masses, in the Army Air Force. When he signed up for officer's training school, she tried to sabotage his application.[86]

Alan was ultimately promoted to captain and served with Army Air Force intelligence, first in London and later in Paris. Dorothy turned fifty in 1943.[87] She was quite fat, and after all the barrels of scotch whiskey and gallons of martinis and cases of

---

get very dirty very quickly, "without seeming to try." Dottie: "I could take John into 21 and leave him at the center table while I went to the ladies' room for no more than a moment, and when I came back, he'd be covered with *tar!*" Bryan recalled the time, during the forties, when Dottie entertained his young children with "the little-known fable" of Aesop and the Wolf: "Well, Aesop was walking through this forest one day, when he came upon a great big wolf caught in a trap. The wolf begged him, 'Please, nice Mr. Aesop, help me out of this cruel trap!' So Aesop did, and when the wolf was free, he bit Aesop on the ankle and said, 'Now go write a fable about *that!*' "

86. Dottie visited Alan in Miami Beach when he graduated from officer's training school in 1942. The Broadway director Joshua Logan also attended the school. Dottie told Logan she was thirsty. After he failed to find any liquor he offered her a bottle of Coca-Cola, which Dottie said she had never tasted. After a few sips, Logan asked if she felt better. "No, but as it was going down I learned a deep, abiding truth about drinking Coca-Cola." What was that? "Never send a boy on a man's errand."

87. At a dinner party during the war, Dottie approached a woman of her own age, but who was dressed and acting like a giddy debutante as she fawned over a clearly uncomfortable army colonel. The woman turned to Dottie: "It's his uniform; I just love soldiers."

Dottie: "Yes, you have in every war."

chain-smoked Chesterfield cigarettes,[88] she was dissipated beyond her years. Her fiction had also deteriorated due to her political radicalization, for she inserted ham-handed diatribes into much of her work, and the best editors, including Harold Ross,[89] grew leery of her. In 1939 she and Alan wrote a play called *The Happiest Man,* but it was too polemical to be commercially produced. In 1944 she wrote her last published verse, a weird piece in *The New Yorker* that forgave soldiers for their wartime affairs.

Dorothy told several friends that she was trying to get into the war herself. Perhaps her application to join the Women's Army Corps was denied because of her age, and perhaps she was not allowed a war correspondent's credential because the government would not issue her a passport due to her subversive background, but perhaps not. Meanwhile, her collected fiction was rereleased by Modern Library, and an anthology[90] of her work was selected by Aleck Woollcott as the fourth in a series of volumes intended for soldiers overseas. It was released stateside by Viking in 1944 as *The Portable Dorothy Parker.*[91] Of the original ten volumes in Woollcott's series, only three have continuously remained in print through the interminably evolving tastes of the last half-century: the Bible, the Shakespeare, and the Parker.

But Dorothy wanted to do more. She started giving speeches and raising funds for worthy causes such as war bonds, the USO, and the Emergency Conference to Save the Jews of Europe. At

88. One time Dottie dropped her cigarette lighter and it bounced under the sofa. Joe Bryan's knees cracked when he kneeled to retrieve it. Dottie smiled, rubbed her hands together, and extended them toward Bryan: "Ah, there's nothing like an open fire——!"

89. There was one particularly stormy argument. Dottie: "When the revolution comes, it will be everybody in the world against Harold Ross!"

90. Dottie did not like anthologists: they were sluggards who liked a comfortable evening at home "raiding a good book."

91. She was living in New York again. In 1945, someone asked why she was hanging around the Viking Press office. Dottie: "Witting for my publisher again." Once she watched Diana and Vincent Sheean's infant daughter toddle through a park: "Isn't it a pity she never married?"

the convention for that last-named group, in July 1943, she passionately appealed for support to assist the removal to Turkey of the four million European Jews she declared were in daily peril of their lives. While the cause was a vital one, and she had even chosen the right side, it emphasized the ambivalence with which she had always regarded her Jewish background. The trauma of her school years had taught her how much of the world regarded Jews. Her usual response had been to obscure her ancestry, which is why some of her acquaintances said that her only happy reminder of her first marriage was the classically Anglo-Saxon surname that allowed her to be "Mrs. Parker." If later in life she would coyly claim that "I was just a little Jewish girl trying to be cute,"[92] she could also write a gratuitously anti-Semitic poem, "The Dark Girl's Rhyme," in 1926, when she was making her reputation. In the thirties she had discovered a new god, the deity of radical socialism, which she still served, yet in the midst of a war that nearly destroyed the world's Jewry, she stood up in active support of their survival. Yet in later years, when Jewish survival of another sort was at stake in the State of Israel, she had no interest.

It would be unfair to conclude that her sudden concern for the Jews during the war was insincere, for though Dorothy often engaged in ill-advised conduct, she was seldom disingenuous. However, she soon reverted to more familiar causes, raising funds for children's books as a member of the National Council of American-Soviet Friendship in 1944 and accepting the acting chairmanship of the Spanish Refugee Appeal, another leftist "anti-fascist" front organization, in 1945.

At the war's end Alan wrote to tell Dorothy that he was involved with another woman, which did not last, but he returned home in late 1946 to a dead marriage. While the details of the

---

92. Near the end of her life, she reluctantly refused to write her autobiography, despite several offers. Dottie: "I'd like to write the damned thing, just so I could call it *Mongrel!*"

legal skirmishing that ensued are unclear, they divorced in Las Vegas in May 1947.[93]

For most of the three years she was divorced from Alan, Dorothy was entangled with Ross Evans, a vastly inferior version of the familiar type.[94] Evans was an alcoholic radio announcer more than twenty years younger than Dorothy, and after he moved into her apartment at a New York hotel he became her writing partner, despite possessing no discernible talent. "They" wrote magazine articles and then a play called *The Coast of Illyria,* which predictably failed. But Dorothy also cowrote the story, though not the shooting script, for the hit movie *Smash-Up—The Story of a Woman.* Dorothy's story of a woman who married a future radio star and later fell into alcoholism earned her an Academy Award nomination and a writing deal with Twentieth Century–Fox for both herself and Evans. After moving back to Hollywood she was told to reduce her drinking,[95] but Evans liked the bottle and eventually deserted her for another woman. Perhaps more damning in Dorothy's eyes, he also stole her dog.

She remarried Alan Campbell three months later, in August 1950.[96] Dorothy cut her hair short and lost most of her excess weight, and things seemed to go well for some months, but then the anticommunist investigations that were heating up put Alan in danger of being blacklisted. He was outraged, because he felt that

93. After the divorce was final, Vincent Sheean tried to cheer Dottie up by telling her he felt sorry for Alan. Dottie: "Oh, don't worry about Alan. Alan will always land on somebody's feet."

94. As Dottie and Evans left a party, a friend of hers complimented his tan. Dottie: "Ah, yes. He has the hue of availability."

95. Evans: "One of her doctors said he didn't like her kidneys and she later confessed that she didn't like his nose." But at Joe Bryan's house in 1949, Bryan asked what she wanted for breakfast. Dottie: "Just something light and easy to fix. How about a dear little whiskey sour?"

96. Dottie coyly pulled the sheet over her face when they woke up the morning of the day of their second marriage: "Mustn't see the bride before the wedding." And at the reception after the wedding: "People who haven't talked to each other in years are on speaking terms again today—including the bride and groom."

he had only got involved in thirties politics because he wanted to make Dorothy happy. There were some nasty fights, and within a year of their remarriage they had again separated.

Dorothy had lambasted the House Un-American Activities Committee during the late forties and she was often threatened with subpoena, but of more sinister import was the visit from the FBI she received in 1951. They wanted to know about her ties to the Communist party, which she denied had ever existed.[97] In truth, though she still occasionally talked like a radical, her political fires had been largely banked on every issue but civil rights some years earlier.[98] Still, that year HUAC cited her and three hundred other writers, artists, actors, and professors for affiliating with communist front organizations. There were no official punitive repercussions.

Others were not so lucky during the fifteen anxious years that followed the Second World War. Though Dies and Thomas and other self-promoters and zealots perpetrated outrages in pursuit of their "investigations," it is also true that many of their targets were or had been communists. Hellman managed to escape through some clever and seemingly courageous testimony, but Hammett and many others went to prison, and some, like Ella and Donald Ogden Stewart, fled to Britain or other countries. Accusations that Dorothy was either a dangerous communist or merely a subversive dupe effectively destroyed what was left of her Hollywood career. She was more or less officially blacklisted through the end of the fifties.

Dorothy was thrilled to move back to New York, and the Volney Hotel on East Seventy-fourth Street, in mid 1952. The Volney and many similar hotels in good East Side neighborhoods housed a large number of older women living alone, and Dorothy and a

97. The federal agents asked if she had conspired to overthrow the United States government. Dottie: "Listen, I can't even get my dog to stay down. Do I look to you like someone who could overthrow the government?"

98. She discussed the thirties more than twenty years later: "They were progressive days. We thought we were going to make the world better—I forget why we thought it, but we did."

younger playwright called Arnaud d'Usseau[99] decided to write a play about those women and their barren and lonely lives. As Dorothy was old, barren, and lonely, she was writing about herself again. They called it *Ladies of the Corridor,* but it was too depressing to succeed. The director, Harold Clurman, suggested cutting a character who committed suicide, leaving the play with a happy ending, but Dorothy refused. It opened in October 1953, to slightly better than mixed reviews. George Jean Nathan thought it was the best play of the year, but it closed after six weeks.

She was again writing short fiction for *The New Yorker,*[100] and in 1957 she started writing book reviews for *Esquire* for six hundred dollars per month. Over the next five years she wrote forty-six book review columns and one short story for the magazine. *Esquire*'s publisher, Arnold Gingrich,[101] paid her whether she wrote her column or not—her work habits had not improved with age—and even gradually raised her salary to seven hundred and fifty dollars a month. She took it because she was sixty-five and had no money. Other projects were considered but later dropped. She wrote one song lyric for the 1956 Leonard Bernstein musical *Candide*. It failed.

Dorothy was at the age when elderly celebrities were often honored for not having died yet,[102] generally by obscure organizations that wanted to burnish their own reputations through the

99. Dottie met Kate and Zero Mostel through d'Usseau. They played Botticelli, a role-reversal game where the "it" player had to deduce an identity through clues given in a question. Dottie's stumper question: "Do you chase men for business and pleasure?" Answer: J. Edgar Hoover.

100. Though Dottie admitted in 1963 that she seldom read the magazine anymore: "It always seems to be the same old story about somebody's childhood in Pakistan."

101. At a dinner, Gingrich was describing himself as "just a simple country boy from Michigan" when he heard the murmur. Dottie: "When convenient."

102. Dottie sat next to the African-American leader W. E. B. Du Bois at his ninety-second birthday celebration in 1960. Some African spear-dancers performed in front of them and, in the course of the dance, thrust their spears increasingly closer to the honoree. Dottie leaned over to Du Bois: "Watch out, mate, or you'll never see ninety-three."

glory reflected by their honorees. She also found herself in demand by those who wanted to hear about the Round Table and the literary twenties. She made recordings and gave readings of her works, and she also sat through several interviews that allowed her to continue her calculated savaging of the Table, its members, and their era, a campaign she had started twenty years earlier when she moved to the left. Of the decade, she admitted: "Damn it, it *was* the twenties and we had to be smarty. I *wanted* to be cute."[103] She said that the Table "was no Mermaid Tavern, I can tell you. Just a bunch of loudmouths showing off, saving their gags for days, waiting for a chance to spring them." In any case, "the only one with any stature who came to the Round Table was Heywood Broun," and that one quickly tired of "their little jokes all about themselves." She still disliked George S. Kaufman, who was "a nuisance and rather disagreeable," though she once admitted that "I guess he was sort of funny," but she also asked, rhetorically, "whoever claimed that he ever said anything funny?" and that he did not "even know what satire is." Kaufman, she concluded, was "a mess."

In early 1961, Dorothy reluctantly reconciled with Alan, again,[104] and they moved back to Los Angeles to work for Charlie Brackett (who had written *Entirely Surrounded* more than a quarter-century before) at Twentieth Century–Fox. They lived in Alan's little West Hollywood bungalow on a one-block street called Norma Place. It was a close-knit community where they became close to Wyatt Cooper, a charming screenwriter in his early thirties.[105]

103. Later in the same interview, Dottie said: "There's a helluva distance between wise-cracking and wit. Wit has truth in it; wise-cracking is simply calisthenics with words."

104. Though still jealous, she doubted that he was sleeping with a notably reserved acquaintance. Dottie: "I know you aren't laying her. If you were, you'd have splinters in your prow."

105. Dottie's tongue never mellowed, even in old age. Cooper recalled how she referred to a woman with a rasping tone: "Doesn't she have the loveliest voice?" Or the way she "flattered" an actor whose huge nose compensated for his lack of any perceptible chin: "Oh, they've been *searching* for a new Cary Grant." (The man actually believed her.)

Dorothy was fired when she did not regularly appear for work. The Campbells survived on unemployment insurance, on occasional payments for television licenses to her old short stories, and on the cash Alan raised by hawking Dorothy's review books, at least until she finally gave up the *Esquire* job at the end of 1962. Dorothy also delivered a few lectures and taught two courses as a celebrity instructor at Los Angeles State College, which turned out badly.

Meanwhile, she and Alan were again drinking heavily and were again at each other's throats. That is, they were until June 14, 1963, when Dorothy found Alan dead in a little hideaway den he had built for himself. He was fifty-nine. The official cause of death was an overdose of the barbiturate Seconal. As Alan was found with a plastic dry-cleaning bag around his head and shoulders, it was not surprising that his death was listed as a probable suicide, although Dorothy and her friends later tried to deny it.[106] Dorothy did not attend the funeral.

As Dorothy turned seventy[107] she was increasingly infirm, suf-

---

A narcissistic neighbor received a small scratch on her face in an auto accident: "I did hope there wouldn't be a scar." Dottie: "As opposed to all those women who *like* looking like they went to school at Heidelberg."

Several celebrities lived in the neighborhood, including the actress Estelle Winwood. Dottie reacted strongly when she was told that Miss Winwood was appearing in the play *Camelot:* "Playing a battlement, no doubt." Another neighbor commissioned a huge painting of himself, seated, with full and detailed frontal nudity that dominated the setting. Dottie professed to admire it: "It's so real, you almost feel he could speak to you, don't you?"

106. When Alan's body was taken away, Dottie was approached by a woman she did not like, identified in one account as June (Mrs. Oscar) Levant. In overly effusive terms, the woman asked what she could do. Dottie: "Get me a new husband."

After a second of shocked silence, the woman sputtered: "I think that is the most callous and disgusting remark I ever heard in my life." Dottie: "So sorry. Then run down to the corner and get me a ham and cheese on rye and tell them to hold the mayo."

107. Dottie is reported to have said two things on that birthday: "Promise me I shall never grow old" and "If I had any decency, I'd be dead. Most of my friends are."

fering from multiple physical problems, including alcoholism,[108] and was nearly blind without her glasses. A few months after Alan's death, she moved back to New York and the Volney. From there she shuttled in and out of hospitals, and then hired a private nurse for several months. Someone suggested she draw up her will, and she bequeathed her estate, which primarily consisted of her copyrights, to Martin Luther King, Jr., and upon his death to the National Association for the Advancement of Colored People. Dorothy had never met Dr. King, but she was extraordinarily impressed by his character and achievements, and the bequest was consistent with her feelings about the single political and moral cause that had always been closest to her heart, that of civil rights.

Although Bea Stewart was again her most trusted friend, Dorothy appointed Lillian Hellman to be her executrix. Bea spent much of her time trying to raise money upon which Dorothy could live, while Dorothy got into the habit of taking whatever royalty and other checks that were sent her, often for sizable amounts, and stuffing them into the backs of bureau drawers. She also reestablished her friendship with Sara Murphy.

In 1965, as Dorothy's health improved, she started to get out again[109] and spent time with Wyatt Cooper and his socialite wife, Gloria Vanderbilt Cooper,[110] who had moved to New York. Dorothy was warily fascinated with society, and vice versa. If she professed reluctance, or even abhorrence, in either the concept or the execution of the institution, she still scrupulously followed the activities of its leaders,[111] who, as it turned out, eagerly

108. During one of her hospital stays, a doctor warned that if she did not stop drinking she would be dead within a month. Dottie sighed: "Promises, promises."

109. It was probably that year that Dottie went with a young man to see an aggressively contemporary play titled *Luv*. After five minutes she turned to him: "I have a feeling you're going to *like* this." And they left.

110. Dottie twitted Gloria's social position, calling her "Gloria the Vth."

111. Around that time Dottie was interviewed by a writer who said that he

wanted to meet her. She was delighted when, in March 1967, the Coopers threw an elegant dinner party in her honor that was attended by much of *tout* New York.[112]

During the afternoon of June 7, 1967, Dorothy suffered a fatal coronary in her Volney apartment. She was seventy-three. The next day the news of her death was reported on the front page and nearly a full jump page of *The New York Times*. Her body was cremated and, after her ashes went unclaimed, they were stored in her attorney's file cabinet for more than twenty years.

Dorothy left a net estate of slightly more than twenty thousand dollars. The murder of Dr. King less than a year after Dorothy's death should have terminated Hellman's executrix authority once she transferred the estate to Dorothy's ultimate legatee, the NAACP, but Hellman went berserk and, without any discernible legal grounds, vigorously defended her right to milk Dorothy's estate. Hellman publicly fumed that "that goddamn bitch" had betrayed her by not leaving Hellman the income from Dorothy's copyrights for the remainder of Hellman's life (she died in 1984). According to Hellman, Dorothy had ostensibly promised to do so because Hellman had supported Dorothy through the last years of Dorothy's life. In fact, Hellman had helped with some matters but had not, by any means, done what she claimed, and in further fact, during those last years Hellman had taken pains to avoid Dorothy and her problems whenever she could. Incidentally, Hellman was later exposed to be a chronic liar of memorable proportions.

In 1972, a court ordered Hellman to turn the estate over to the

---

was soon going to talk with the famous transsexual Christine Jorgenson, who lived on Long Island with her mother. Dottie asked if he had met Christine's mother; the writer admitted he had not, and wondered why she wanted to know. Dottie: "Because I'd be very interested in knowing what sex she is."

112. At the Cooper party, a guest admired the wineglasses: "I always think that wine tastes so much better in lovely glasses, don't you?" Dottie: "Oh, yes. Paper cups aren't right."

NAACP, but in an interview with Nora Ephron[113] the next year Hellman argued, with wondrous presumption, that her legal position should have been vindicated because of her superior political virtue: "It's one thing to have real feeling for black people, but to have the kind of blind sentimentality about the NAACP, a group so conservative that even many blacks now don't have any respect for, is something else. She must have been drunk when she did it. I was executor, you know."

In a letter he drafted a few weeks after Dorothy's death, the eminent *New Yorker* writer E. B. White issued the accepted verdict on Dorothy Parker's professional legacy: "Seen in perspective, though, some of the well-loved figures of those days have shrunk with the passage of time. Dotty Parker died on Page 1, but except for a handful of sterling short stories her contribution to letters was slight and she herself knew that she was not much of a poet." Yet, as W. H. Auden astutely observed, "some books are undeservedly forgotten, none are undeservedly remembered." Why is Dorothy Parker so peculiarly memorable? Why do her verses stay in print, decade after decade, when the works of so many of her critically preferred contemporaries, even "serious" poets such as Edna St. Vincent Millay and Elinor Wylie, are less prominent? Is it another symptom of an insidious vulgarization of High Culture, or is it something else? Though merit and popularity clearly are distinguishable qualities, are they also contradictory?

Nearly thirty years have passed since Dorothy Parker's death. In that time she has been instated as a sort of minor but resilient historical figure, somewhat literary but not exclusively so, known

113. Nora Ephron's screenwriter parents, Phoebe and Henry Ephron, socialized with Dottie in Hollywood. Once Dottie was at their house for a game of anagrams. The writer Sam Lauren came up with "currie." Dottie insisted there was no such word. Phoebe Ephron settled the dispute with a jar of Crosse and Blackwell "currie" powder. Dottie: "What do they know? Look at the way they spell 'Crosse.'"

for a time and a taste but not for any one thing in particular. In a 1995 *Commentary* magazine essay, the eminent lit crit warhorse Hilton Kramer supplied a useful accounting for the architect Philip Johnson; it is an appraisal that may also apply to Dorothy:

> There are certain figures in the arts who, although minor in accomplishment and equivocal in their aesthetic influence, are so completely representative of the spirit of their age that they come to occupy a historical position far greater than the intrinsic merits of their work could ever justify.

Beyond her own nine books, Dorothy has been the gist of dozens of newspaper and magazine articles, four book-length biographies, an eponymic period murder mystery, a feature film, a postage stamp, and hundreds of entries in quotation and anecdote collections, which may cumulatively act to keep us interested, but not to make us aware. In an affectionate 1968 *Esquire* profile of Dorothy, Wyatt Cooper concluded: "If you didn't know Dorothy Parker, whatever you think she was like, she wasn't. Even if you did know her, whatever you thought she was like, she probably wasn't." And that is that.

Dorothy wrote more than 330 poems and free verses in the thirty years from 1915. She published nearly three hundred of these during the twenties, an average of more than one poem or free verse every two weeks. It was a prolific but necessary achievement, because the poems and verses were her primary source of income, at least until she became Constant Reader in 1927.

Dorothy originally published these poems and verses in at least twelve newspapers and magazines: first in *Vanity Fair* (1915–19, 1926) and *Vogue* (1916), then in *Life* (1920–27), *The Saturday Evening Post* (1922–23), Frank Adams's Conning Tower in *The World* (1923–31) and later the *New York Herald Tribune* (1931–35), *The New Yorker* (1925–44), and the *Bookman* (1927–28). She also published single pieces in *The New Republic* and *McCall's* (both in 1927) and the *Yale Review* (1930), and she even wrote a rhyme for a Simon and Schuster advertisement that appeared in the *Saturday Review of Literature* in 1931. At least two of her pieces were unpublished. Most of her pieces appeared in *Life* (129), The Conning Tower (70), *The New Yorker* (60),*Vanity Fair* (22), and *The Saturday Evening Post* (19). She was probably paid for all of them except the Conning Tower and the unpublished pieces, and she collected most of them—more than two hundred in all—in her three books of original poetry and two subsequent compilations. The other 122 poems and free verses—the forgotten ones—are collected here for the first time.

Some of the scholars who studied Dorothy Parker have referred to these pieces; a few have even extracted from them. But the vastly greater proportion of these works have not been in print since they originally appeared in those newspapers and magazines between 1915 and 1938. Some of the biographers have speculated about why Dorothy did not include these pieces in her earlier collections. The consensus is that she was embarrassed by some of her earlier, and implicitly inferior, work. The publisher of one of her compilations once delicately suggested that she had not included "some" verses from her earlier collections because they were "no longer to her taste."

There is some truth to that. The earlier works are, on the whole, more lighthearted and ephemeral. They tend to be more exuberant and are less refined. Taken as a whole, they possess less artistic merit. But Dorothy also used other criteria for her selections—and rejections. As was stated earlier, at some length, she was trying to project a certain image (even retitling and editing many of her poems before collecting them), and many of her earlier works did not help her in that regard. She apparently was not allowed to use any of the nineteen verses she had published in *The Saturday Evening Post*, which retained its copyrights. Dorothy reportedly was blackballed by that magazine for ridiculing the publisher George Horace Lorimer's friends, and perhaps some years later there was a desire to get more revenge by refusing her permission to reprint. And perhaps some of the poems that ran in other publications recalled unpleasant or embarrassing memories that were better left undisturbed; pieces like "A Musical Comedy Thought," with its terrifying accusation of plagiarism; or "To Elspeth," and its vulgar tinges of refuted envy.

But whatever Dorothy's motivations may have been, there is reason to appreciate the work she chose to leave behind. It is more eclectic. It is breezier. And it is vastly less self-conscious. Most of these pieces appeared during the early to mid twenties, a hectic time when Dorothy often submitted a poem nearly every week, which forced her to cast around for ideas wherever she could. Some of the pieces dissected current fads, such as the slang-spewing "Invictus" or "The Passionate Freudian to his Love"; some profiled current celebrities, such as "Lynn Fontanne" or "*Life*'s Valentines"; others marked various annual celebrations, such as "Christmas, 1921" or "Paging St. Patrick." Some were more personal and explored subjects that ranged from her love of animals ("To My Dog"), to her precarious financial situation ("Song for the First of the Month"), to what was becoming her particular obsession, the perils of evanescent love ("Lyric").

These previously uncollected pieces also contain nearly all of Dorothy's experiments in structured poetic forms, including her first triolet (a short poem with a rhyme scheme of *ab, aa, abab*; with the first line repeated as the fourth and seventh lines, and the second line repeated as the eighth); sonnet (a fourteen-line poem, usually in iambic pentameter, that fully expresses a single thought or sentiment in either of two rhyme schemes: she preferred the Italian, with an octave followed by a sestet, to the English, with three quatrains followed by a couplet); and ballade (usually a three-stanza poem with identical rhyme schemes, followed by an envoi, and with each of the stanzas and the envoi having the same final line). She also attempted the rondeau (a ten- or thirteen-line poem on two rhymes, with the opening words repeated twice as unrhymed refrains).

Dorothy gloried in new language and was, in her own way, an

important historical resource. In her very first poem, "Any Porch" (September 1915), she referred to Irene Castle's "bobbed hair"; in February 1921's "Invictus," she "said a mouthful"; six months later, in her Movies hate verse, she talked about "sex appeal"; and in April 1922 she colloquially called "The Glad Girl" a "moron." According to the most authoritative reference, the second edition of *The Oxford English Dictionary*, in each instance Dorothy's citation is the first known use of the word or phrase. And there are several more, but "what the hell," there is no point in listing them all.

The hate verses are a particularly rich and amusing source of contemporaneous references. For example, in her harangue against Slackers, which was published in the heady days of late 1917, when the United States was officially in the First World War but not yet really bloodied by it, Dorothy indicted the Conscientious Objectors, whom she judged "the real German atrocities," and the Pacifists, "who will do anything on earth to have peace except go out and win it"; but in an ironic anticipation of her own destiny she also pilloried the Socialists, "the Professional Bad Sports" who "don't want anybody to have any fun." (Less than a year later, in her diatribe against Bohemians, she attacked "The Table D'Hôte Bolsheviki. They are always in revolt about something. Nothing has been done yet that they can wholly approve of.")

In her June 1921 tirade against Parties, she fulminated against obnoxious card-players before finally observing "yet they shoot men like Elwell." Richard Elwell was a noted bridge authority who had been mysteriously murdered the previous year. Later in 1921, in that scrutiny of Movies, Dorothy reflected the emerging and ultimately endemic New Yorker's envy of Hollywood salaries, when she described the big Hollywood actress who "supports an indulgent husband in the style to which he has become accustomed; the wages of sin is $3,500 a week."

Those precarious undertakings called "art" are considered and judged through intensely personal yet hazy prisms of emotion, taste and experience. This collection will ultimately be measured on those grounds. Enjoy.

The
Poems

(And Some "Modernist Verse")

THE BRIDGE FIEND

How do we cut for the deal?
> That's so, we did it before.
Partner, we'll beat them, I feel—
> Oh, I just hate keeping score!
Really, I don't understand,
> Under the line or above?
Partner, just *look* at my hand!
> I must be lucky at love.

Partner, I haven't a thing—
> The hearts were dealt in a lump.
Don't tell me that was *your* king—
> Well, then, I've wasted a trump.
Now it's my bid, I suppose—
> Goodness, who dealt me this mess?
You made it lilies on *those?*
> Isn't it time to progress!

Oh, did you see what you did?
> Why, you're an absolute dub!
Didn't you hear what I bid?
> *Couldn't* you lead me a club?
Kindly keep track of what's played—
> What a remarkable lead!
Tell me how many we made—
> Set us three hundred? Indeed!

ANY PORCH

"I'm reading that new thing of Locke's—
      So whimsical, isn't he? Yes—"
"My dear, have you seen those new smocks?
      They're nightgowns—no more, and no less."

"I don't call Mrs. Brown *bad,*
      She's *un*-moral, dear, not *im*moral—"
"Well, really, it makes me so mad
      To think what I paid for that coral!"

"My husband says, often, 'Elise,
      You feel things too deeply, you do—'"
"Yes, forty a month, if you please,
      Oh, servants impose on *me,* too."

"I don't want the vote for myself,
      But women with property, dear—"
"I think the poor girl's on the shelf,
      She's talking about her 'career.'"

"This war's such a frightful affair,
      I know for a fact, that in France—"
"I love Mrs. Castle's bobbed hair;
      They say that *he* taught her to dance."

"I've heard I was psychic, before,
      To think that you saw it—how funny—"
"Why, he must be sixty, or more,
      I told you she'd marry for money!"

"I really look thinner, you say?
        I've lost all my hips? Oh, you're *sweet*—"
"Imagine the city to-day!
        Humidity's *much* worse than heat!"

"You never could guess, from my face,
        The bundle of nerves that I am—"
"If you had led off with your ace,
        They'd never have gotten that slam."

"So she's got the children? That's true;
        The fault was most certainly his—"
"You know the de Peysters? You *do?*
        My *dear,* what a small world this is!"

THE GUNMAN AND THE DÉBUTANTE
A Moral Tale

A wild and wicked gunman—one who held a gang in thrall—
    A menace to the lives of me and you,
Was counting up, exultingly, the day's successful haul—
    As gunmen are extremely apt to do.
A string of pearls, a watch or two, a roll of bills, a ring,
    Some pocketbooks—about a dozen, say—
An emerald tiara—oh, a very pretty thing!
    Yes, really, quite a gratifying day.

A dainty little débutante came trippingly along,
    With wistful, trusting eyes of baby blue;
She softly hummed a fragment of a most Parisian song—
    As débutantes are very apt to do.
That wild and wicked gunman felt he couldn't miss the chance
    To end his busy day triumphantly;
"Though scarcely in the habit of attacking débutantes,
    Your money or your life, my dear," said he.

The dainty little débutante was trembling with alarm,
    Appealingly she looked him through and through,
And laid her helpless little hand upon his brawny arm—
    As débutantes are very apt to do.
Then earnestly she prayed the wicked gunman to be good,
    She begged that he'd reform that very day;
Until he dropped his wicked gun, and promised that he would,
    And bade her go her sweet and harmless way.

The wild and wicked gunman sat considering it all.
     "At last," he cried, "I've met my Waterloo";
He vowed he'd give to charity the day's successful haul—
     As gunmen are extremely apt to do.
But when he tried to find his gains and give to those in want—
     The pocketbooks, the watches, bills and ring—
He found, to his amazement, that the little débutante
     Had taken every solitary thing!

THE LADY IN BACK

I don't know what her name is, for you see we've never met;
 I don't know if she's dark, or if she's fair;
I don't know if she's young or old, or rich or poor—and yet
 Whatever place I chance to go, she's there.
I don't know where she came from, and I don't know where she'll go;
 Why fate has linked our lives I cannot see,
The world's so full of people—oh, I'd really like to know
 Why must she *always* sit in back of me?

She's always right on duty when I go to see a play—
 Unfailingly, she's seen that play before,
And so she tells what's coming, in her entertaining way—
 For me, the drama holds surprise no more.
"Now watch, the husband enters, as I told you that he would,
 At first you'll think he'll shoot her, but he'll not.
And later she goes back to him, and says that she'll be good"—
 Obligingly she thus unfolds the plot.

When I am at the opera, of course she's sure to come.
 She there adopts another policy—
The more familiar arias she feels obliged to hum,
 And always just a trifle off the key.
But when the singers reach those heights to which she can not climb—
 Oh, then I plumb the very depths of gloom!
For, lest I be too happy, she will occupy that time
 By long accounts of who's in love with whom.

I never can avoid her at the humble picture show,
        Of course, the film is always one she's seen
Reliable as Mary's lamb, she's right behind, I know,
        Revealing all the secrets of the screen.
When heroes tumble over cliffs, as movie heroes will,
        And villains blow up bridges, just for fun,
I know that she takes pleasure in extinguishing my thrill
        By telling just exactly how it's done.

I really couldn't tell you if she's widow, maid, or wife;
        I've never heard about her family;
I don't know who appointed her to take the joy from life,
        I can't imagine what she sees in me.
I often sit and think of it, and wonder why it's so,
        Why, every place that I am, she is too,
The whole wide world to choose from—oh, I'd really like to know
        Why can't she *sometimes* sit in back of you?

OH, LOOK—I CAN DO IT, TOO

Showing That Anyone Can Write Modernist Verse

BACCHANALE

Hand in hand, we ran through the Autumn forest;
Our laughter soaring on the wings of the mad wind;
In and out, tracing a fantastic path,
Through the passionate, flaming dogwood
And the slim, virginal birches,
Our limbs flashing white against the riotous background.
The grape-leaves I twined rested lightly on your hair,
And, as we ran, you shouted snatches of wild songs—
Pagan hymns of praise to the dead gods.
On we rushed, dizzy with the strong wine of Autumn. . . .
I wonder if you were married, too.

SUNDAY

A litter of newspapers
Piled in smothering profusion.
Supplements sprawling shamelessly open,
Flaunting their lurid contents—
"Divorced Seven Times, Will Re-Wed First Wife,"
Unopened sheets of "help" advertisements;
Editorials, crumpled in a frenzy of ennui;
Society pages, black with lying photographs.
Endless, beginningless heaps of newspapers. . . .
Outside, a thin gray rain,
Falling, falling hopelessly,
With a dull monotony of meaningless sound,
Like the voice of a minister reading the marriage service.

THE PICTURE GALLERY

My life is like a picture gallery,
With narrow aisles wherein the spectators may walk.
The pictures themselves are hung to the best advantage;
So that the good ones draw immediate attention.
Now and then, one is so cleverly hung,
That, though it seems unobtrusive,
It catches the most flattering light.
Even the daubs are shown so skillfully
That the shadows soften them into beauty. . . .
My life is like a picture gallery,
With a few pictures turned discreetly to the wall.

FRAGMENT

We came face to face in the crowd;
Hemmed all about by pushing, straining figures,
Berserk with the thought of getting home to dinner.
Heavy about us rose the odor of crowded humanity,
Hot in our ears sounded their polyglot curses.
But the crowd was kind, for it pushed you into my arms,
There you rested, one supreme moment,
Your delicate body quivering with exquisite timidity.
We stood, we two alone, on the pinnacle of rapture,
Our souls throbbing together.
Then we were torn apart.
But Hope leaped high within me,
For, before you were borne away from me,
You whispered a few shy syllables—
The answer to my feverish question. . . .
Why did you give me the wrong telephone number?

LETTER TO ROBERT BENCHLEY

Roughing It in the Country at The Birches, Maine

Greetings to all from the pine-scented woods!
We hope everybody is feeling so good.
Kindly forgive our writing in pencil;
It's too much trouble to get the other utensil.
We want to tell you about this place.
With us it certainly stands like an ace.
To-day we went out on the lake to fish;
That you were with us, was our heartiest wish.
We caught a trout, not to mention some chubbs,
And then put them back, like a couple of dubs.
A salmon then got on the line by mistake,
But we put him back, for the little ones' sake.
The lake at times is fairly rough.
We go out upon it, though.
The water is cold and full of salmon,
And the scenery hereabouts is charming.
Our Septoline has given out—
We're better off, there's not a doubt.
But still, we'd like a dash of hootch,
In fact, we'd like it very much.
As yet, we have not been in bathing,
We're waiting for a warmer occasion.
We're saving our bathing-suits, crisp and new,
To give to some Ziegfeld ingenue.
The trail around the island's fine;
To-day we saw some porcupines.
The tennis court is a perfect whale;
We thought at first it was part of the trail.
The Wallace Frye just broke a shaft—
You should have heard the captain laugh!
Some children here have the whooping-cough.
If we don't get it, we'll be in soft.

The desk clerk's manner is proud and airy,
Nevertheless, we think he's a fairy.
There are some people right next door
Who turned out to be a terrible bore.
There always seems to be some kind of a hitch
Isn't Nature a (finish this line for yourself, and
    get a year's subscription to the Boston Post.)
The captain's trousers may be out at the seat;
But he stands ace-high with Mr. Bradstreet.
He should worry about cash in hand,
He's got a rating of 800 thou*sand*.
Each time the boat sails, he's on her
To collect 54 cents from each passenger.
We expect to be back on Sunday noon,
Or if not then, some fine day soon.
We'll return to the city, 'mid sighs and tears,
With vacation over for another year.
We're feeling fine—the same to you,
And now it's late, we must say adieu.
We think of you all, on the Biltmore roof
And wish you were with us, that's the God's truth.
We watch the flickering firelight,
And wonder if Duggie and Robby are tight.
In the firelight glow, so cheery and warm,
We weep over the mortgage on the Benchley farm.
And now we cannot write any more,
So, once again, we must say au revoir.

OUR OWN HOME TALENT

Miss Isadora Quigley pays
      Terpsichore devotion;
In rhythmic bliss, she bends and sways—
      The true *vers libre* of motion.
She blithely bounds o'er field and stream,
      Attired with Greek simplicity,
And gives, the while, her basic scheme
      A lot of free publicity.
Her genius is, as all agree
      Who watch her do her dances,
An infinite capacity
      For taking awful chances.

You may not care for it—but there!
It keeps her in the open air.

The name of Mr. Eustace Young,
      Our author, sharp and Shavian,
Some day will be on every tongue—
      Including Scandinavian.
He has, he's often told, a *flair*
      For tense and throbbing crudity;
On every page his soul lies bare,
      In literary nudity.
Already he is hailed as great
      By cultural minorities,
For all his works have been, to date,
      Suppressed by the authorities.

Our *literati* have confessed
Nothing succeeds like the suppressed.

Now art Miss Iris Blount employs;
   Her batik and her stencil
Express her maiden griefs and joys,
   She swings a wicked pencil!
In forms of cube and octagon,
   Ignoring technicalities,
She splashes her impressions on,
   In broadest generalities.
She paints no view of moonlit glen,
   No landscape, green and grassy;
Her subjects run to gentlemen
   And ladies, in their chassis.

Her art, our connoisseurs imply,
Is all in the beholder's eye.

To down all kings and presidents
   Our Mr. Tench proposes;
His loudly uttered sentiments
   Are redder than the roses.
He urges anarchism's cause
   In terms concise, but notable;
And what he says about the laws
   Would scarcely pass as quotable.
He pleads that marriages be few,
   While love be free, in plenty—
Which last endears him greatly to
   The local *cognoscenti*.

His word is law, among our set,
On rules of sovietiquette.

WITH BEST WISHES

Glad Christmas Day once more has come—
        There's little novelty in that.
It's welcomed eagerly by some, .
        Which isn't to be marveled at.
Their stockings hold a house and lot
        (I hope you gather what I mean),
A picturesquely furnished yacht.
        A next year's model limousine,
A sable wrap of graceful cut,
        A sheaf of cheques for vast amounts;
It's not the thought that matters, but
        The gift which goes with it that counts.

But I'LL get a multitude of seasonable cards,
        A bowl full of lily bulbs, approaching their decease;
A pair of gilded shoe-trees, with appropriate regards,
        And a leather-bound "Evangeline," with colored frontispiece.

It's scarcely any wonder that
        The season finds me all unmoved,
For Father Christmas leaves me flat—
        Step-Father Christmas, it has proved.
'Twas ever thus—from early youth
        I've seen my hopes decay, because
Too soon I learned the bitter truth:
        There isn't any Santa Claus.
Each Yuletide mocks my touching trust;
        The give and let give is my plea,
It's Christmas Day for some, but just
        December twenty-fifth for me.

For I'LL *get a paper-weight, to crush my Christmas cheer,*
  A hand-painted needle-case, a brace of button-hooks,
A host of cordial wishes for a prosperous new year,
  And a holiday edition of the "Rubaiyat," de luxe.

I've often heard that some there are—
  How hard such tales are to believe!
To prove that costlier by far
  It is to give than to receive.
On Christmas they present their friends
  With motor cars, and pearls in strings,
And blocks of stock with dividends,
  And other useful little things.
Though I have no such benefits,
  I sing the Christmas spirit's praise.
I know the giver's thrill—for it's
  A poor Yule which won't work both ways.

So I'LL *give a laundry bag, of chintz refined, yet gay;*
  A tooth-brush container of a fanciful design,
A flock of timely greetings for a snappy Christmas Day,
  And a highly colored copy of "That Old Sweetheart of Mine."

INVICTUS

Farthest am I from perfection's heights,
      Faulty am I as I well could be,
Still I insist on my share of rights.
      When I am dead, think this of me:
Though I have uttered the words "Yea, bo,"
      Though I use "ain't" to get a laugh,
Though I am wont to explain "Let's go,"
      Though I say "You don't know the half"—
Black through my record as darkest jet,
      Give me, I beg, my devil's due;
Only remember, I've never yet
      Said, "How's the world been treating you?"

"What could be sweeter?" I fondly muse;
      "You said a mouthful," I confess;
Witnesses testify that I use
      "Yes, indeedy," in times of stress;
"Oh, it's a great life," I loudly claim—
      "If you don't weaken," I amend;
"I'll tell the world," is my middle name;
      "Well, how's the boy?" I greet a friend.
While I acknowledge each grave defect,
      Still I am master of my fate—
All that I ask you is, Recollect
      I never said, "I'm here to state."

"Yours till hell freezes," I sign my mail;
      "I'll say it is," I coyly cry;
"What's the good word?" is my cheery hail;
      Bidding farewell, I say "Bye-bye";
I demand, "How do you get that way?"
      "Oh, have a heart," is all my plea;
Speaking of oysters, I sadly say,
      "I like them, but they don't like me."

Humbly I own to each one of these,
      Yet I atone for all my slips;
Heap me a measure of credit, please—
      "Kiddie" has never passed my lips.

A MUSICAL COMEDY THOUGHT

My heart is fairly melting at the thought of Julian Eltinge;
    His vice versa, Vesta Tilley, too.
Our language is so dexterous, let us call them ambi-sexterous—
    Why hasn't this occurred before to you?

SONG OF THE OPEN COUNTRY

When lights are low, and the day has died,
I sit and dream of the countryside.

Where sky meets earth at the meadow's end,
    I dream of a clean and wind-swept space
Where each tall tree is a stanch old friend,
    And each frail bud turns a trusting face.
A purling brook, with each purl a pray'r,
    To the bending grass its secret tells;
While, softly borne on the scented air,
    Comes the far-off chime of chapel bells.
A tiny cottage I seem to see,
    In its quaint old garden set apart;
And a Sabbath calm steals over me,
    While peace dwells deep in my brooding heart.

And I thank whatever gods look down
That I am living right here in town.

THE PASSIONATE FREUDIAN TO HIS LOVE

Only name the day, and we'll fly away
    In the face of old traditions,
To a sheltered spot, by the world forgot,
    Where we'll park our inhibitions.
Come and gaze in eyes where the lovelight lies
    As it psychoanalyzes,
And when once you glean what your fantasies mean
    Life will hold no more surprises.
When you've told your love what you're thinking of
    Things will be much more informal;
Through a sunlit land we'll go hand-in-hand,
    Drifting gently back to normal.

While the pale moon gleams, we will dream sweet dreams,
    And I'll win your admiration,
For it's only fair to admit I'm there
    With a mean interpretation.
In the sunrise glow we will whisper low
    Of the scenes our dreams have painted,
And when you're advised what they symbolized
    We'll begin to feel acquainted.
So we'll gaily float in a slumber boat
    Where subconscious waves dash wildly;
In the stars' soft light, we will say good-night—
    And "good-night!" will put it mildly.

Our desires shall be from repressions free—
     As it's only right to treat them.
To your ego's whims I will sing sweet hymns,
     And *ad libido* repeat them.
With your hand in mine, idly we'll recline
     Amid bowers of neuroses,
While the sun seeks rest in the great red west
     We will sit and match psychoses.
So come dwell a while on that distant isle
     In the brilliant tropic weather;
Where a Freud in need is a Freud indeed,
     We'll be always Jung together.

LOVE SONG

Suppose we two were cast away
      On some deserted strand,
Where in the breeze the palm trees sway—
      A sunlit wonderland;
Where never human footstep fell,
      Where tropic love-birds woo,
Like Eve and Adam we could dwell,
      In paradise, for two.
Would you, I wonder, tire of me
      As sunny days went by,
And would you welcome joyously
      A steamer? . . . So would I.

Suppose we sought bucolic ways
      And led the simple life,
Away—as runs the happy phrase—
      From cities' toil and strife.
There you and I could live alone,
      And share our hopes and fears.
A small-town Darby and his Joan,
      We'd face the quiet years.
I wonder, would you ever learn
      My charms could pall on you,
And would you let your fancy turn
      To others? . . . I would, too.

Between us two (suppose once more)
        Had rolled the bounding deep;
You journeyed to a foreign shore,
        And left me here to weep.
I wonder if you'd be the same,
        Though we were far apart,
And if you'd always bear my name
        Engraved upon your heart.
Or would you bask in other smiles,
        And, charmed by novelty,
Forget the one so many miles
        Away? . . . That goes for me.

IDYL

Think of the things that can never come true—
     Save in the shadowy country of dreams.
Think of what might be, for me and for you,
     Could we but shatter the world's sorry schemes.
Think of our own little vine-covered nest;
     Each day, at sunset, I'd wait for you there,
Down by the gate, in the glow of the west,
     Dressed all in white, with a rose in my hair.

Think of a chair, softly-cushioned and wide;
     Think of a hearth, where the red firelight dies;
Think of me sitting there, close by your side,
     Reading the stories writ deep in your eyes.
Think of the years, like an unending song,
     Think of a quiet we never have known.
While, all forgotten, the world rolls along,
     Think of us two, in a world of our own.

Now that you've thought of it seriously—
Isn't it great that it never can be?

ABSENCE

I never thought that heav'n would lose its blue
      And sullen storm-clouds mask the gentle sky;
I never thought the rose's velvet hue
      Would pale and sicken, though we said good-by.
I never dreamed the lark would hush its note
      As day succeeded ever-drearier day,
Nor knew the song that swelled the robin's throat
      Would fade to silence, when you went away.

I never knew the sun's irradiant beams
      Upon the brooding earth no more would shine,
Nor thought that only in my mocking dreams
      Would happiness that once I knew be mine.
I never thought the slim moon, mournfully,
      Would shroud her pallid self in murky night.
Dear heart, I never thought these things would be—
      I never thought they would, and I was right.

TO MY DOG

I often wonder why on earth
    You rate yourself so highly;
A shameless parasite, from birth
    You've lived the life of Reilly.
No claims to fame distinguish you;
    Your talents are not many;
You're constantly unfaithful to
    Your better self—if any.
Yet you believe, with faith profound,
    The world revolves around you;
May I point out, it staggered 'round
    For centuries without you?

In beauty, you're convinced you lead,
    While others only follow.
You think you look like Wallace Reid,
    Or, at the least, Apollo.
The fatal charms with which you're blest,
    You fancy, spell perfection;
The notion, may I not suggest,
    Is open to correction?
An alien streak your tail betrays;
    Your ears aren't what they would be;
Your mother was—forgive the phrase—
    No better than she should be.

One can but feel your gaiety
  Is somewhat over-hearty;
You take it on yourself to be
  The life of every party.
In bearing, while no doubt sincere,
  You're frankly too informal.
And mentally, I sometimes fear,
  You're slightly under normal.
The least attention turns your brain,
  Repressions slip their tether;
Pray spare your friends the nervous strain
  And pull yourself together!

You take no thought for others' good
  In all your daily dealings,
I ask you, as a mother would,
  Where *are* your finer feelings?
I think I've seldom run across
  A life so far from lawful;
Your manners are a total loss,
  Your morals, something awful.
Perhaps you'll ask, as many do,
  What I endure your thrall for?
'Twas ever thus—it's such as you
  That women always fall for.

LYRIC

How the arrogant iris would wither and fade
    If the soft summer dew never fell.
And the timid arbutus that hides in the shade
    Would no longer make fragrant the dell!
All the silver-flecked fishes would languish and die
    Were it not for the foam-spangled streams;
Little brooks could not flow, without rain from the sky;
    Nor a poet get on without dreams.

If the blossoms refused their pale honey, the bees
    Must in idleness hunger and pine;
While the moss cannot live, when it's torn from the trees,
    Nor the waxen-globed mistletoe twine.
Were it not for the sunshine, the birds wouldn't sing,
    And the heavens would never be blue.
But of all Nature's works, the most wonderful thing
    Is how well I get on without you.

FULFILMENT

I do not sit and sigh for wealth untold,
      It never thrusts itself into my schemes;
I shrink from all your piles of clanking gold—
      Better my sparkling hoard of golden dreams.
A life of limousined and jeweled ease
      Is but a round of fathomless *ennui*.
Your motor cars, your pearls, your sables—these
      Are naught to me.

Better a homely flat in Harlem's wilds
      Than a costly living's spurious benefits;
Better a simple butter-cake at Childs'
      Than caviar and stalled ox at the Ritz.
Your unearned gold, to me, is shot with flaws;
      A life of honest toil I'd make my lot—
Which really makes it very nice, because
      It's what I've got.

SONG FOR THE FIRST OF THE MONTH

Money cannot fill our needs,
      Bags of gold have little worth:
Thoughtful ways and kindly deeds
      Make a heaven here on earth.
Riches do not always score,
      Loving words are better far.
Just one helpful act is more
      Than a gaudy motor car.
Happy thoughts contentment bring
      Crabbed millionaires can't know;
Money doesn't mean a thing—
      Try to tell the butcher so!

None can stretch his life an hour
      Though he offer boundless wealth:
Money, spite of all its pow'r,
      Cannot purchase ruddy health.
Simple pleasures are the best,
      Riches bring but misery,
Homely hearts are happiest,
      Joy laughs loud at poverty.
Pity those in Mammon's thrall,
      Poor, misguided souls are they,
Money's nothing, after all—
      Make the grocer think that way!

Greatest minds the world has known
      All agree that gold is dross
Man can't live by wealth alone;
      Bank books are a total loss.
Banish strife and greed and gloom,
      Throw off money's harsh control,
Sow good deeds, and watch them bloom—
      Hyacinths, to feed the soul.
Hoard no pelf, lest moth and rust
      Do their work and leave you flat.
Money? It is less than dust—
      Laugh the landlord off with that!

LYNN FONTANNE

Dulcy, take our gratitude,
       All your words are golden ones.
Mistress of the platitude,
       Queen of all the old ones.
You, at last, are something new
       'Neath the theatre's dome. I'd
Mention to the cosmos, you
       Swing a wicked bromide.

Heroines we've known, to date,
       Scattered scintillations
(Courtesy the Wilde estate)
       Through their conversations.
Polished line and sparkling jest—
       They've provided plenty.
Dulcy's bromides brought us rest—
       Dulcy far niente.

TO MARJORIE RAMBEAU

In "Daddy's Gone A-Hunting"

If all the tears you shed so lavishly
    Were gathered, as they left each brimming eye.
And were collected in a crystal sea,
    The envious ocean would curl up and dry—
So awful in its mightiness, that lake,
    So fathomless, that clear and salty deep.
For, oh, it seems your gentle heart must break,
    To see you weep.

We try to tell ourselves it isn't true,
    We strive to feel that dawn must follow dark,
We strain to hold the thought that, off-stage, you
    Are happy as the widely-mentioned lark.
But, though you wring our feelings to their cores,
    Our devastated hearts you seem to keep,
For, oh, we pack the theatre to its doors
    To see you weep.

CHRISTMAS, 1921

I do not ask you for presents rare,
     Other-world trove of forgotten metals;
Orchids that opened to jungle air,
     Tropical hate in their writhing petals;
Onyx and ebony, black as pain,
     Carved with a patience beyond believing;
Perfumes, to harry the startled brain;
     Laces that women have died in weaving;
Cool-tinted pearls from the ocean, where
     Grottoes of dolorous green regret them.
I do not ask you for presents rare—
     Dearest, I know that I wouldn't get them.

Give me your love, on this Christmas Day.
     Give me your thoughts, when the chimes are ringing.
Send me the happier along my way,
     Deep in my soul let your words be singing.
Give me your wishes, as bells sound clear,
     Charming the air with their golden measure.
Give me your hopes for the unborn year,
     Fill up my heart with a secret treasure.
Give me the things that you long to say,
     All of your tenderest dreams unfetter.
Give me your love, on this Christmas Day—
     But come across, please, when times get better.

MARILYN MILLER

From the alley's gloom and chill
      Up to fame danced *Sally*.
Which was nice for her, but still
      Rough upon the alley.
How it must regret her wiles.
      All her ways and glances.
Now the theatre owns her smiles,
      Sallies, songs, and dances.

Ever onward *Sally* goes—
      Life's one thing that's certain.
O'er the end of other shows
      Let us draw a curtain.
Their untimely ends are sad,
      But they stood no chances,
For, you see, they never had
      Sally's songs and dances.

FRAGMENT

Why should we set these hearts of ours above
   The rest, and cramp them in possession's clutch?
Poor things, we gasp and strain to capture love,
   And in our hands, it powders at our touch.
We turn the fragrant pages of the past,
   Mournful with scent of passion's faded flow'rs,
On every one we read, "Love cannot last"—
   So how could ours?

It is the quest that thrills, and not the gain,
   The mad pursuit, and not the cornering:
Love caught is but a drop of April rain,
   But bloom upon the moth's translucent wing.
Why should you dare to hope that you and I
   Could make love's fitful flash a lasting flame?
Still, if you think it's only fair to try—
   Well, I am game.

FIGURES IN POPULAR LITERATURE

THE SHEIK

The desert chieftain here behold,
  The Dempsey of the Nile.
He knocks the lady readers cold
  And cramps their husbands' style.
The heroine reels back for more.
  They play like happy kids—
He tells his love, then knocks her for
  A row of pyramids.

She revels in his gallant deeds;
  Her passions higher mount
Each time he languidly proceeds
  To drop her for the count.
They marry in the end—they do
  In all such compositions—
And now, no doubt, he'll knock her through
  Another twelve editions.

So if you'd knock the ladies dead,
Just use your right and go ahead.

THE FLAPPER

The playful flapper here we see,
  The fairest of the fair.
She's not what Grandma used to be—
  You might say, *au contraire.*

Her girlish ways may make a stir,
        Her manners cause a scene,
But there is no more harm in her
        Than in a submarine.

She nightly knocks for many a goal
        The usual dancing men.
Her speed is great, but her control
        Is something else again.
All spotlights focus on her pranks,
        All tongues her prowess herald,
For which she may well tender thanks
        To God and Scott Fitzgerald.

Her golden rule is plain enough—
Just get them young and treat them rough.

THE DRAB HEROINE

There was a time, as doubtless you're
        Enabled to recall,
When heroines of literature
        Were not like this at all.
Their hair was heaped in glinting curls,
        Their forms were wondrous fair,
And when it came to sex, the girls
        Admittedly were there.

To-day, toward woolen lingerie
        The lady's thoughts are turned,
And sex is in its infancy
        So far as she's concerned.

A kitchen drudge, whom all ignore,
    She leads a life entrancing
As Cinderella's was, before
    She took up ballroom dancing.

Abandon hope, and learn to cook,
And you will figure in a book.

THE WESTERN HERO

This hero ranks among the best—
    He's Nature's rugged child.
You've heard about the woolly West?
    'Twas he who drove it wild.
Observe that he is dressed to kill
    (Forgive the pun, I pray),
In pranks like this he finds a thrill—
    He's simply full of play.

In his revolver terrors lurk;
    His aim's a deadly one.
Could Annie Oakley see his work,
    She'd throw away her gun.
He trifles not with woman's love,
    In spite of his virility,
For he's a charter member of
    The natural nobility.

He shoots to kill and aims to please;
Our books are filled with such as these.

THE GLAD GIRL

This child of curious tendencies
        To your acquaintance add.
Her smile is permanent, for she's
        The gladdest of the glad.
Come battle, famine, flood, or fire,
        The cheery little one
Accepts it as her heart's desire,
        And says, "Ain't we got fun?"

The joy of living fills her cup;
        Of hope, she's never rid.
Imagine how she'd brighten up
        Your household—God forbid!
The bitter ills her fortunes send
        She sprinkles smiles galore on;
It seems to me our little friend
        Is something of a moron.

But if I had her author's pelf,
I'm sure that I'd be glad, myself.

THE BOY SAVANT

Behold, in all his native state,
        Dispensing truths profound,
The gifted undergraduate,
        The learned campus hound.

His reading fills his youthful head
        With thoughts that throb and hum,
For Nietzsche, as is often said,
        Abhors a vacuum.

In lighter moments, he's the man
        That fills the flappers' dreams;
He'd make the All-American—
If there were petting teams.
His self-regard is scarcely small,
        His conversation shows it;
Just ask him anything at all—
        For he's the boy that knows it.

Oh, youth verbose, our feelings spare—
For God, for country, and forbear!

THE GREAT LOVER

I'm sure you've met this lad before;
        His work is fast, though rough.
He feels that all is fair in war—
        In love, it's fair enough.
His tale the Vice-Suppressor takes,
        And drinks in every word
(A single swallow never makes
        A Sumner, we have heard).

Our hero lived in ages gone—
          The days of bright romance.
We read about his goings-on
          And sigh, "So this is France!"
You must concede, the boy was good
          Among the local ladies;
But his intentions toward them would
          Not pave the streets of Hades.

How sweet to read of days of old
When knights, to say the least, were bold!

CHANTEY

A wet sheet and a straining sail,
  And a sea of shifting blue;
A wide sky and a rousing gale,
  And joy in the heart of you;
A clean line, where the sky hangs low
  And a seagull soars and dips;
And the old voice that bids men go—
  Go down to the sea in ships.

So go and sail the gold sea, the bold sea, the cold sea;
The waving, craving, raving sea that's fringed with silken foam;
Oh, go and sail the green sea, the keen sea, the mean sea—
But if it's all the same to you, I'll stick around at home.

The swift turn of the night-wind's whim,
  And the tang of hempen strings;
The sharp snap of the halyards slim,
  And the spray that cuts and stings.
The wild chorus the breezes hum,
  And the waves that prowl and creep;
And the old voice that bids men come—
  Come over the tameless deep.

So go and sail the white sea, the light sea, the bright sea,
The dashing, crashing, smashing sea, that dances in the gale;
Go on and sail the sad sea, the bad sea, the mad sea—
But if it's just the same to you, I'd rather be in jail.

MORAL TALES FOR THE YOUNG [1]

Maude, the brightest of the sex,
Forged her daddy's name to checks,
Took them to the local banks,
Cashed them, with a smile of thanks.
All the money came in handy—
Maudie was so fond of candy!
Weight she gained in way affrighting,
So she's given up her writing.

Save the money, when you forge;
Little ladies do not gorge.

Don, the little apple-cheek,
Sold his aunt's blue-ribbon Peke,
Sneaked it out of Auntie's house,
Hidden in his sailor blouse.
Donald planned to spend his earnings
Gratifying all his yearnings.
But the chance for pleasure slipped him,
For the doggie's buyer gypped him.

If they can't complete the deal,
Nicer children do not steal.

LIFE'S VALENTINES

PRINCESS MARY AND VISCOUNT LASCELLES

Here behold, and likewise lo,
Princess Mary and her beau.
Bright her cheek with maiden blush;
Shall we say a royal flush?
How we've watched their love's ascents
In the Sunday supplements!
Blessings for the happy pair;
For their photographs—the air!

MR. DAVID WARK GRIFFITH

Look, and you will surely find
Right above, the Master Mind.
(Just a nickname of his own
Which he worked up all alone.)
He it was who made, they say,
Movies what they are to-day;
This the goal for which he's tried—
Lord, I hope he's satisfied!

DAVID BELASCO

Often in the local press
On your kindness you lay stress.
Love's the basis of your art,
So you say—that is, in part.
Frequently you tell us of
How devotedly you love
Actors, public, critics, too . . .
Echo answers, "Yes, you do."

CALVIN COOLIDGE

"Ah," we said; and eke "At last.
Things won't be as in the past;
Once vice-presidents were nil,
But our Fighting Calvin will
All such precedents destroy."
"Ah," we said; and "Atta boy!" . . .
Now we wonder dolefully
What's become of Calvin C.?

DR. FRANK CRANE

Daily you distribute praise
'Mong clean books and wholesome plays.
Honest toil and hard-earned gold,
Kindness to the weak and old;
Where would all the virtues be
Without such publicity?
Wealth untold you're paid, per line,
Won't you be my Valentine?

AVERY HOPWOOD

How you must have loved, when small,
Chalking words upon a wall!
"Ladies' Night" we owe to you,
"Getting Gertie's Garter," too.
Gaily gath'ring royalties
On your bedroom phantasies,
Ever heavier grows your purse
As you go from bed to worse.

FLORENZ ZIEGFELD

Still we're groggy from the blow
Dealt us—by the famous Flo;
After 1924,
He announces, nevermore
Will his shows our senses greet—
At a cost of five per seat.
Hasten, Time, your onward drive—
Welcome, 1925!

JOHN WANAMAKER

On the advertising page
Scintillates our dry good sage.
Not a text that Honest John
Cannot write a sermon on.
Readers live from day to day
Just to see what he will say.
"Have you seen his last?" they cry.
"Would to God I had," says I.

THE FAR-SIGHTED MUSE

Dark though the clouds, they are silver-lined;
> *(This is the stuff that they like to read.)*
If Winter comes, Spring is right behind;
> *(This is the stuff that the people need.)*
Smile, and the World will smile back at you;
> Aim with a grin, and you cannot miss;
Laugh off your woes, and you won't feel blue.
> *(Poetry pays when it's done like this.)*

Whatever it is, is completely sweet;
> *(This is the stuff that will bring in gold.)*
Just to be living's a perfect treat;
> *(This is the stuff that will knock them cold.)*
How could we, any of us, be sad?
> Always our blessings outweighing our ills;
Always there's something to make us glad.
> *(This is the way you can pay your bills.)*

Everything's great, in this good old world;
> *(This is the stuff they can always use.)*
God's in His heaven, the hill's dew-pearled;
> *(This will provide for the baby's shoes.)*
Hunger and War, do not mean a thing;
> Everything's rosy, where'er we roam;
Hark, how the little birds gaily sing!
> *(This is what fetches the bacon home.)*

PAGING SAINT PATRICK

The good Saint Patrick, in his day,
    Performed a worthy act:
He up and drove the snakes away,
    With more technique than tact.
Could he descend from realms above
    And roam about New York,
He'd find it reminiscent of
    The good old days in Cork.
The snakes he knew could never tie
    The brand our village has—
The kind that daily multiply
    And thrive on tea and jazz.

Should he his tales of snakes relate
    We'd strive to hide a laugh;
For, though the saint was wise and great,
    He didn't know the half.
Where'er he'd go, to dine or dance,
    Or lunch, or tea, or sup,
The saint would have a splendid chance
    To do some cleaning up.
Could he but leave his present star,
    He'd see that things were changed—
How sad such little visits are
    Not easily arranged!

MOOD

Unless I yield my love to you, you swear
  In strangely distant countries must you dwell;
Denied this heart of mine, you could not bear
  These dear, familiar scenes we've loved so well.
To-morrows that will come, you could not face
  With only pain to bear you company,
Among the whispering memories of this place,
  The little, intimate things that speak of me.

Where mighty mountains rear their cruel height,
  The world between us, would you dwell, apart;
Where curious peace, that comes with tropic night,
  Answers the bitter question of your heart.
The lilac bush, that bends with bloom in May,
  The winding path, the arbor where we sat.
These things should know you nevermore, you say—
  Ah, love, if I could only count on that!

TRIOLETS

Herewith I send you my heart,
    Marking it "Fragile—don't break it."
Rather a radical start—
Herewith I send you my heart;
Take it, I beg, in good part
    (That is, assuming you'll take it).
Herewith I send you my heart,
    Marking it "Fragile—don't break it."

Take me, or let me alone—
    What, after all, does it matter?
Ever my feelings you've known;
Take it, or let me alone—
Though, I might readily own,
    I'd recommend you the latter.
Take me, or let me alone—
    What, after all, does it matter?

Sweet, I have waited too long;
    Heedless and wanton I've tarried.
Silenced forever my song—
Sweet, I have waited too long.
Bitter the hemlock, and strong—
    Now you have gone and got married!
Sweet, I have waited too long;
    Heedless and wanton, I've tarried.

TO MYRTILLA, ON EASTER DAY

Myrtilla's tripping down the street,
    In Easter finery.
The Easter blooms are not more sweet
    And radiant-hued than she.
The rarest woodland violets were
    Less fragrant than her frills,
The sunny-tinted hair of her
    Would shame the daffodils.
Ah, many a heart-beat halts and skips,
    And sighs pursue her way,
As down the street Myrtilla trips,
    This joyous Easter Day.

Myrtilla's tripping gaily by,
    In Easter garb arrayed.
Ah, would the lads as deeply sigh
    For any other maid?
The lads, they come from far and near,
    When down the street she starts;
Oh, lightly step, Myrtilla dear,
    Your path is strewn with hearts.
The maids are held in envy's grips,
    For they are left, forlorn,
As down the street Myrtilla trips,
    This glorious Easter morn.

Ah, well may echo, sweet as love,
          Her laugh's delicious lilt,
For sure she knows the power of
          Her Easter bonnet's tilt;
A master wrought, with tender care,
          Each dainty frill and flounce;
The fragrance of her, cool and rare,
          Costs thirty-five per ounce.
Parisian rouge defines her lips,
          And pearls her throat bedeck—
As down the street Myrtilla trips,
          I hope she breaks her neck!

POEM IN THE AMERICAN MANNER

I dunno yer highfalutin' words, but here's th' way it seems
When I'm peekin' out th' winder o' my little House o Dreams;
I've been lookin' 'roun' this big ol' world, as bizzy as a hive,
An' I want t' tell ye, neighbor mine, it's good t' be alive.
I've ben settin' here, a-thinkin' hard, an' say, it seems t' me
That this big ol' world is jest about as good as it kin be,
With its starvin' little babies, an' its battles, an' its strikes,
An' its profiteers, an' hold-up men—th' dawggone little tykes!
An' its hungry men that fought fer us, that nobody employs.
An' I think, "Why, shucks, we're jest a lot o' grown-up little boys!"
An' I settle back, an' light my pipe, an' reach fer Mother's hand,
An' I wouldn't swap my peace o' mind fer nothin' in the land;
Fer this world uv ours, that jest was made fer folks like me an' you
Is a purty good ol' place t' live—say, neighbor, ain't it true?

FANTASY

Did we love each other, sweetest,
    Skies would be forever blue;
Time would flutter by on fleetest
    Wings of glittering golden hue.
Joy beyond a poet's telling
    Should we learn the meaning of;
Arcady would be our dwelling—
    Did we love.

Did we love each other, darling,
    Banished ugliness and gloom;
Ever sweet would pipe the starling,
    Ever gay the rose would bloom.
Care and trouble could not find us,
    Bliss untold would be our lot.
But, one scarcely need remind us,
    We do not.

MORAL TALES FOR THE YOUNG [2]

Little Gormley stole a purse.
Took it from his crippled nurse.
It was quite a lucky touch—
She'd been saving for a crutch.
So our hero, for a starter,
Bought a seat for "Gertie's Garter."
Spent in vain his gains unlawful—
For he thought the show was awful!

When *you* plunder Nursie's hoard.
Spend it where you won't be bored.

Gracie, with her golden curls,
Took her mother's string of pearls.
Figuring—as who would not?
It would pawn for quite a lot.
Picture, then, her indignation
When she found it imitation!
Though her grief she tries to smother,
Grace can't feel the same towards Mother!

All pretence and sham detest;
Work for nothing but the best.

Earnest—such a little man!
Got his family's sedan.
Drove it over hill and dale—
Just escaped the county jail—
Maimed, in his exhilaration,
Folk of spotless reputation.
But his trip with gloom was tainted—
Now the car must be repainted!

Strive to keep the death-rate low—
Think how high repair bills go!

THOUGHTS

Yes, my love, I think about you
    In the morning's roseate flush;
Heavy hang the clouds, without you,
    Sullen seems the dawning's blush.
In the slender, graceful grasses,
    Silver-tipped with sparkling dew,
In the woodland's shadowy masses
    All that I can see is you.

When the noon-day sun is burning,
    Hot the scented air, and clear,
Then to you my thoughts are turning,
    And I would that you were here.
Then I dream that, happy vagrants,
    We are wandering hand in hand
Through the lanes of light and fragrance
    Into Summer's fairyland.

When the weary sun is sinking,
    And the blossoms close, in rest,
Then of you, my love, I'm thinking,
    As I watch the brilliant west.
When the little stars show faintly
    In the Maxfield Parrish sky,
When the moon gleams, cold and saintly,
    Then to you my fancies fly.

When the frightened owls are calling,
    And the sombre midnight reigns,
Thick and fast the shades come crawling,
    Like the thoughts of fevered brains,
When life trembles at the brink of
    Death's unfathomable deep,
You're the last thing that I think of—
    Goodness knows, I need some sleep.

MEN I'M NOT MARRIED TO

No matter where my route may lie,
   No matter whither I repair,
In brief—no matter how or why
   Or when I go, the boys are there.
On lane and byway, street and square,
   On alley, path and avenue,
They seem to spring up everywhere—
   The men I am not married to.

I watch them as they pass me by;
   At each in wonderment I stare,
And "But for heaven's grace," I cry,
   "There goes the guy whose name I'd bear!"
They represent no species rare,
   They walk and talk as others do;
They're fair to see—but only fair—
   The men I am not married to.

I'm sure that to a mother's eye
   Is each potentially a bear;
But though at home they rank ace-high,
   No change of heart could I declare.
Yet worry silvers not their hair;
   They deck them not with sprigs of rue.
It's curious how they do not care—
   The men I am not married to.

  L'Envoi
In fact, if they'd a chance to share
   Their lot with me, a lifetime through,
They'd doubtless tender me the air—
   The men I am not married to.

WOODLAND SONG

The hothouses' offerings, costly and rare,
      Cannot ape the forget-me-not's blue;
Blooms forced to perfection can't hope to compare
      With the lowly anemone's hue.
The humble wild rose, unassuming and meek,
      Must have stolen the setting sun's glow;
The blushes which play o'er its delicate cheek
      Are of tints that no palette may know.

No matter how lovely these flowers may be,
Gardenias and orchids look better to me.

The purple-eyed violet, fragrantly cool,
      Spends its beauty extravagantly.
The waxen-white lily that sleeps on the pool
      Gives its loveliness lavishly free.
Their glorious petals the poppies unfold
      For whoever may happen to pass,
And Nature, made mad by the buttercups' gold,
      Flings it wantonly over the grass.

But my favorite blossoms, I'm here to aver,
Are American Beauties at five dollars per.

RONDEAU [1]

It isn't fair, to me, when you're away.
In vain the clouds their brightest hues display.
      Sweet Summer dons in vain her gladdest guise—
      The vision falls but coldly on my eyes;
The sky seems draped in melancholy gray.

Though never bloomed the roses half so gay,
Though never half so radiant shone the day,
      This loveliness my stubborn heart denies;
        It isn't fair.

And do you, also, sing a minor lay?
Do you to bitter yearnings fall a prey?
      "Well, no," frank Echo honestly replies,
      "In fact, it is distinctly otherwise."
And that, my dear, is why again I say
        It isn't fair.

ROSEMARY [1]

Ah, no, I dare not lose myself in dreams
     Of that dead day we ne'er shall know again;
So pitifully brief a while it seems,
     So sharp the thought of you, as you were then.
The poignant memories of little things—
     A flower in your coat, a frock I wore;
The wistful autumns, and the troubling springs—
     I dare not let them come to me once more.

The tender gloamings, when we two would stray
     Where locusts hung their frothy blooms above;
The violets—like my eyes, you used to say;
     The rustic bridge, where first you spoke of love;
The words we whispered, while the summer breeze
     Fluttered the grasses with its scented breath;
Ah, no, I dare not summon thoughts like these;
     I'm so afraid I'd laugh myself to death.

DAY-DREAMS

We'd build a little bungalow,
      If you and I were one.
And carefully we'd plan it, so
      We'd get the morning sun.
I'd rise each day at rosy dawn
      And bustle gaily down;
In evening's cool, you'd spray the lawn
      When you came back from town.

A little cook-book I should buy,
      Your dishes I'd prepare;
And though they came out black and dry,
      I know you wouldn't care.
How valiantly I'd strive to learn,
      Assured you'd not complain!
And if my finger I should burn,
      You'd kiss away the pain.

I'd buy a little scrubbing-brush
      And beautify the floors;
I'd warble gaily as a thrush
      About my little chores.
But though I'd cook and sew and scrub,
      A higher life I'd find;
I'd join a little women's club
      And cultivate my mind.

If you and I were one, my dear,
      A model life we'd lead.
We'd travel on, from year to year,
      At no increase of speed.
Ah, clear to me the vision of
      The things that we should do!
And so I think it best, my love,
      To string along as two.

SONG [1]

And shall we build a little nest
    In Arcady, in Arcady,
Where we can settle down and rest
    In sweet security;
A place where sunbeams cast their spell,
    And shadows play, and shadows play,
Where you and I and Love can dwell
    Forever and a day?

And shall we go there, you and I,
    In poppy time, in poppy time,
When fluffy cloudlets dot the sky
    And clustered roses climb?
And shall we watch the seasons wane,
    And come and go, and come and go,
And welcome April's golden rain,
    And hail December's snow?

And will no other ever find
    Our garden spot, our garden spot?
And shall we leave the world behind
    And count it well forgot?
There boundless peace can come to us,
    But trouble can't, but trouble can't.
And shall we live forever thus?
    You bet your life we shan't.

GRANDFATHER SAID IT

When I was but a little thing of two, or maybe three,
My granddad—on my mother's side—would lift me on his knee;
He'd take my thumb from out my mouth and say to me: "My dear,
Remember what I tell you when you're choosing a career:

> "Take in laundry work; cart off dust;
> Drive a moving van if you must;
> Shovel off the pavement when the snow lies white;
> But think of your family, and please don't write."

When I was two I cannot say his counsel knocked me cold.
But now it all returns—for, darling, I am growing old,
And when I read the writing of the authors of today
I echo all those golden words that grandpa used to say:

> "Clean out ferryboats; peddle fish;
> Go be chorus men if you wish;
> Rob your neighbors' houses in the dark midnight;
> But think of your families, and please don't write."

MONODY

Slowly the roses droop and die;
      (Where is the love we knew of old?)
Slowly the sun-bright days go by.
      (Little white love, so cold, so cold.)
Dark are the leaves on the weary ground,
      Sad are the winds in the still, gray glen;
Slowly the year goes its listless round
      Over again.

Somewhere the sunbeams dance and play;
      (Where is the love that used to thrill?)
Somewhere the riotous roses sway.
      (Little white love, so still, so still.)
Somewhere the skies of young April shine
      Bright as the heavens we prayed to then . . .
Somewhere you're pulling the same old line
      Over again.

SOMEWHAT DELAYED SPRING SONG

Crocuses are springing,
Birds are lightly winging,
Corydon is singing
  To his rustic lute;
Sullen winter passes,
Shepherds meet their lasses,
Tender-tinted grasses
  Shoot.

All the world's a-thrilling,
Meadow larks are shrilling,
Little brooks are trilling,
  You, alone, are mute;
Why do you delay it?
Love's a game—let's play it,
Go ahead and say it—
  Shoot!

SONNET [1]

Sweeter your laugh than trill of lark at dawn.
      As marble richly gleams, so shines your throat.
The grace of you would shame the pale young fawn;
      Rather than walk, like silken down you float.
Lighter your touch than fall of April rain;
      Cooler your cheek than petal washed with dew.
Whene'er you speak, all gladness and all pain
      Speak also, in the throbbing voice of you.

Like blossom on its stem is poised your head,
      Wrapped closely round about with fragrant bands.
As roses' passionate hearts, your mouth is red;
      Like lilies in the wind, your long white hands.
Brighter the glance of you than summer star;
      But, lady fair, how awful thick you are!

TO A LADY

Lady, pretty lady, delicate and sweet,
    Timorous as April, frolicsome as May,
Many are the hearts that lie beneath your feet
    As they go a-dancing down the sunlit way.

Lady, pretty lady, blithe as trilling birds,
    Shy as early sunbeams play your sudden smile.
How you quaintly prattle lilting baby words,
    Fluttering your helpless little hands the while!

Lady, pretty lady, bright your eyes and blue,
    Who could be a-counting all the hearts they broke?
Not a man you meet that doesn't fall for you;
    Lady, pretty lady, how I hope you choke!

MEMORIES

Once, you say, we felt love's blisses
    When the world was not so wise;
Once, you say, you knew my kisses
    Under Babylonian skies.
There fulfilled our scorching passion,
    There we pledged our tender vow—
Strange we meet in this cold fashion
    Here and now.

Maybe you were, as you've stated,
    Fooling round in Babylon;
Maybe you participated
    In the local goings-on.
Maybe things like that befell you,
    Ages past. But anyhow,
I was never there, I'll tell you
    Here and now.

PROMISE

Love beyond my maddest dreaming
    You have sworn you'll show to me;
You will guide me to the gleaming,
    Reeling heights of ecstasy.
Dizzier joy than else could reach me,
    Fiercer bliss and wilder thrill,
All of this some day you'll teach me,
    Y-e-e-s you will!

RONDEAU [2]

Give me a rose, cool-petaled, virgin white,
Pure as the morning, mystical as night;
      Not bold gardenias, flaunting their expense
      Like courtesans, in perfumed insolence,
Nor brazen orchids, feverishly bright.

Give me no hothouse violets, cold, polite,
With lengths of costly ribbon girdled tight—
      Matrons, in corseted magnificence;
            Give me a rose.

One girlish blossom proffer as your mite.
Ah, lovelier by far within my sight
      Than rich exotics' glamorous pretense
      Is one shy rose, sweet in its diffidence.
And then besides, my love, the price is right;
            Give me a rose.

SONG OF THE CONVENTIONS

We'd dance, with grapes in our wind-tossed hair,
    And garments of swirling smoke;
We'd fling wild song to the amorous air,
    Till the long-dead gods awoke.
Our quivering bodies, young and white,
    Poised light by the brooklet's brink,
We'd whirl and leap through the moon-mad night—
    But what would the neighbors think?

We'd bid the workaday world go hang,
    And idle the seasons through;
We'd pay no tribute of thought or pang
    To the world that once we knew.
With hearts in ecstasy intertwined,
    In languorous, sweet content,
We'd leave all worry and care behind—
    But how would we pay the rent?

We'd roam the universe, hand in hand,
    Through tropical climes, or cold,
And find each spot was a wonderland,
    A country of pearl and gold.
Our hearts as light as the sunlit foam,
    We'd voyage the oceans o'er,
With never a thought for those at home—
    But wouldn't our folks be sore?

SONG [2]

Clarabelle has golden hair,
        Mabel's eyes are blue,
Nancy's form is passing fair,
        Mary's heart is true.
Chloë's heart has proved to be
        Something else again;
Not so much on looks is she
        But she gets the men.

Doris deals in verse and prose,
        Stella's brow is high,
Martha, swift and skillful, sews,
        Maud can bake a pie.
Chloë neither sews nor cooks,
        Cannot swing a pen,
Doesn't seem to run to books;
        She just gets the men.

Winnie's gayly dancing feet
        Fly on fairy wings;
Silver bells ring, clear and sweet,
        When Belinda sings.
Fair and true and talented
        Are they all—but then
Little Chloë knocks them dead;
        Chloë gets the men.

BALLADE OF UNDERSTANDABLE AMBITIONS

Fame and honor and high degree,
      Jeweled scepter and throne-room plot—
Yellow primroses, they, to me;
      Milder longings are mine, God wot.
Smooth and simple, I'd have my lot;
      I'd depart on another tack.
At my aim give me just one shot—
      All I want is a lot of jack.

Fond communion with field and tree,
      Bread and cheese in an ivied cot;
Sweet and clean though the thought may be,
      I subscribe to it ne'er a jot.
Other yearnings my heart make hot,
      Other cravings my spirit rack.
In my dreams to my goal I trot—
      All I want is a lot of jack.

On the pages of history
      Ne'er my name shall I sign and blot;
I'll go down to posterity
      Neither scholar nor patriot.
Cloaks of Shelley and Keats and Scott
      Ne'er will fall on my humble back;
Immortality ask I not—
      All I want is a lot of jack.

L'Envoi

Prince, or Rover, or Rex, or Spot,
      Ere I die let me take a crack
At the wish which I've never got—
      All I want is a lot of jack.

"HOW BOLD IT IS"

How bold it is, this fine young love we bear;
A high, white flame, to cut the ghostly night;
A virgin armor, burnished hard and bright
To turn the blows of age and death and care!
Too brave a thing it is, to see it break
Beneath the unending taps of little things—
Of sharpened words, and hurried answerings,
And fretful illness, and recited ache,
And tiny jealousies, and whimpering woe,
And household plannings, year on futile year,
And patient "Yes, my love," and "Yes, my dear,"
And "Why did you do thus, and why do so?"

Quick, let us part, that ever our love may be
As now we know it, young and bold and free.

SONG OF A CONTENTED HEART

All sullen blares the wintry blast;
      Beneath gray waves the waters sleep.
Thick are the dizzying flakes and fast;
      The edged air cuts cruel deep.
The stricken trees gaunt limbs extend
      Like whining beggars, shrill with woe;
The cynic heavens do but send,
      In bitter answer, darts of snow.
Stark lies the earth, in misery,
      Beneath grim winter's dreaded spell—
But I have you, and you have me,
      So what the hell, love, what the hell!

The wolf, he crouches at the sill,
      And, grinning, bares expectant fangs,
While heavy o'er the house, and chill,
      The coming of the landlord hangs.
Each moment, on the shrinking door,
      May sound his knocking's hideous din.
And more and more, and ever more,
      The eager bills come trooping in.
The milkman clamors for his due,
      The grocer and the cook, as well—
But you have me, and I have you,
      So what the hell, love, what the hell!

SONG OF THE WILDERNESS

We'll go out to the open spaces,
        Break the web of the morning mist,
Feel the wind on our upflung faces.
        [This, of course, is if you insist.]
We'll go out in the golden season,
        Brave-eyed, gaze at the sun o'erhead.
[Can't you listen, my love, to reason?
        Don't you know that my nose gets red?]
Where the water falls, always louder,
        Deep we'll dive, in the chuckling foam.
[I'll go big without rouge and powder!
        Why on earth don't you leave me home?]

We'll go out where the winds are playing,
        Roam the ways of the brilliant West.
[I was never designed for straying;
        In a taxi I'm at my best.]
Minds blown clean of the thoughts that rankle,
        Far we'll stray where the grasses swirl.
[I'll be certain to turn my ankle;
        Can't you dig up another girl?]
We'll go out where the light comes falling—
        Bars of amber and rose and green.
[Go, my love, if the West is calling!
        Leave me home with a magazine!]

TRIOLET [1]

Give back the heart that I gave;
      Keeping it never can mend it.
See, I can smile, and be brave.
Give back the heart that I gave,
Hold it no more as your slave—
      I've got a new place to send it.
Give back the heart that I gave;
      Keeping it never can mend it.

WANDERLUST

I want to go out to the woodlands green,
    And stand 'neath the mighty trees.
I'm longing to hark to the mournful keen—
    The voice of the wistful breeze.
I'll find me the place where the fox-gloves start,
    And violets coyly bloom,
Where the whispering cypress stands apart
    In mystical, fragrant gloom.
I'll go where the feathery grasses lean
    To gaze in the placid brook;
I want to go out to the woodlands green,
    And never give them a look.

I want to go down to the open sea;
    I'll search for a sunlit strand
Where clean-scented winds blow cool and free
    O'er glittering, swirling sand.
I want to go out on the sparkling shore
    Where frolicsome wavelets play;
I'm yearning to feel on my cheek, once more,
    The kiss of the ardent spray.
There's longing, down deep in the heart of me,
    To look on the sun-shot foam.
I want to go down to the open sea—
    And then I'll come right back home.

I want to go back to a country town,
      Afar from the city's thrills—
A dear little village that's snuggled down
      Asleep, by the guardian hills.
I'm going to stand in the ancient square
      And look to the crimson west
When pealing of chimes, on the quiet air,
      Bids villagers go to rest.
I'm yearning to dress in a gingham gown
      And play with a frisking calf.
I want to go back to a country town,
      And give it a hearty laugh.

A TRIOLET

You'll be returning, one day.
  (Such premonitions are true ones.)
Treading the dew-spangled way,
You'll be returning, one day.
I'll have a few things to say—
  I've learned a whole lot of new ones.
You'll be returning, one day.
  (Such premonitions are true ones.)

PÆAN

The sun shines fair, the sun shines true,
    The sun shines golden bright;
The sky takes on a lovelier blue,
    The clouds a daintier white.
The birds trill out a roundelay,
    The rosebuds dance with glee,
Each living thing holds holiday;
    The world belongs to me!

My heart beats loud, my heart beats strong,
    My heart beats fast and high;
Within my soul's a rousing song,
    A light within my eye.
Go, raise the banners high in air,
    And spread the tidings round!
Let drums and trumpets boom and blare,
    For I have lost a pound!

SONG [3]

When summer used to linger,
    Before the daisies died,
You'd but to bend your finger
    And I was by your side.
And, oh, my heart was breaking,
    And, oh, my life was through;
You had me for the taking;
    "Now run along," said you.

But now the summer's over,
    The birds have flown away,
And all the amorous clover
    Has turned to sober hay.
And you're the one to tarry,
    And you're the one to sigh,
And beg me, will I marry.
    "The deuce I will," say I.

AND OBLIGE

When I've made a million dollars—it may take a year or two
    At the present rate of speed that things are going—
There are various little matters that are somewhat overdue,
    And the prospect, at the moment, isn't glowing;
But as soon as I've a million, as I started in to say,
    Life will be, I take it, gloriously happy;
For already I am planning to expend it in a way
    That will be, if I may say it, rather snappy.

I will charter me a taxicab of cheery white and brown,
    And you'll never catch me glancing at the meter!
And I'll make a little tour of all the milliners in town;
    And the question is, Could anything be sweeter?
Just for stamps and lunch and cigarettes, each morn I'll draw a check
    For a thousand dollars, payable to bearer,
And you'll hear the pearls a-clanking, as I drape them on my neck.
    It occurs to me that little could be fairer.

It is true that a million doesn't take you very far,
    And it's hard to find another when you've shot it;
But I'll blow it like the widely known inebriated tar,
    For I want to be a good one while I've got it.
So the minute I've a million, I'll go right ahead and spend,
    Though it doesn't last me more than over Sunday.
In the meantime, though, I wonder, as a favor to a friend,
    Could you let me have a dollar—say, till Monday?

TRIOLET [2]

It is never the cost of the gift;
      It is the thought that I treasure.
Such affections as mine do not shift.
It is never the cost of the gift—
Which is quite an incentive to thrift;
      Business must come before pleasure.
It is never the cost of the gift;
      It is the thought that I treasure.

BALLADE OF A NOT INSUPPORTABLE LOSS

Who will slacken the mental strain,
      Who'll sit down and explain to me.
This, the riddle that racks my brain,
      This, the theme of my monody?
      I'm a glutton for mystery—
Plots and puzzles to me are clear;
      Just one thing has me up a tree—
Where did the flappers disappear?

What's become of that mighty train.
      All so carefully bold and free.
Each like each, as were drops of rain.
      Short of garment, and frank of knee?
      Do they flap in eternity?
All I know is, they are not here;
      To the riddle, I hold no key—
Where did the flappers disappear?

Think not, reader, that I'd complain.
      Squander on me no sympathy.
Though they've vanished, I feel no pain—
      I get on—rather swimmingly.
      I'd not cavil at Fate's decree;
Rather, give it a rousing cheer,
      Still, there's something I cannot see—
Where did the flappers disappear?

L'Envoi
Prince, you've labored incredibly
      Tracing the snows of yesteryear;
Answer this one, and let that be—
      Where did the flappers disappear?

SONG OF A HOPEFUL HEART

Oh, time of our lyrical laughter,
    Oh, pageant of glittering days,
The glamourous Aprils—and after,
    The delicate, mystical Mays!
So gallant and sudden and heedless,
    So gayly defiant of regret,
We smiled as we thought how 'twas needless
    To vow that we'd never forget
Those galloping days of our blisses,
    Alike, and yet never the same—
But you have forgotten my kisses,
    And I have forgotten your name.

Oh, always there's one who remembers,
    Who brightens, with memories' glow,
The ponderous, sullen Novembers,
    The colorless Winters, and slow.
Why linger in shadowy sadness?
    Why drape us in lavender hue?
The red of that magical madness
    Our hearts could be wearing anew.
It's only the coward who misses
    The glorious rush of the game—
Try hard to remember my kisses;
    I guess I can think of your name.

SONG [4]

When all the world was younger.
      When petals lay as snow.
What recked I of the hunger
      An empty heart can know?
For love was young and cheery,
      And love was quick and free;
To-morrow might be weary,
      But when was that to me?

But now the world is older,
      And now to-morrow's come.
The winds are rushing colder,
      And all the birds are dumb.
And icy shackles fetter
      The brooklet's sunny blue—
And I was never better;
      But what is that to you?

SONG FOR AN APRIL DUSK

Tell me tales of a lilied pool
    Asleep beneath the sun.
Tell me of woodlands deep and cool,
    When chuckling satyrs run.
Tell me, in light and tinkling words,
    Of rippling, lilting streams.
Tell me of radiant-breasted birds,
    Who sing their amorous dreams.
Tell of the doomed butterfly
    That flings his hour away.
Fated to live and love and die
    Before the death of day.

Tell me tales of the moon-pale sprites
    Whose beauty none may know.
Tell me of secret, silver nights
    When great red stars are low.
Tell of the virgin Spring, the fair,
    Who roams the circling years.
Rain-drops strung in her fragrant hair,
    Her eyes a-mist with tears.
Tell me of elves, who leap to kiss,
    Who trip the velvet sward.
Tell me stories of things like this,
    And, boy, will I be bored!

ROSEMARY [2]

I wear your fragrant memory, like a spray of mignonette,
    As I tread the winding ribbon of the years.
How clear the radiant image of you stands before me yet
    In the thousand little mirrors of my tears.
And ah, my dearest love, when I forget the way to dream
    I'll forget your silent nearness in the dark,
Where languorous lilies floated on a quiet woodland stream—
    Or were you the one I'd meet in Central Park?
The love of you was sudden and the heart of you was strong;
    There were leaping little devils in your eyes;
Your laughter rode the morning like a joyous May-day song—
    No, I guess that must have been two other guys.

Could I forget your April smile, the shining way of you,
    Could I forget your method so adroit?
Could I forget those stories of the other girls you knew?
    Or was that the butter-and-egg man from Detroit?
A pair of truant children, we would often steal away
    Where the city's voice was gloriously mute,
And plan the little cottage we should have, one happy day—
    Or were you the boy that had the wife in Butte?
You had my first, my golden love, and though we're torn apart,
    Through all the circling years, I've been the same.
Your name is ever written on the pages of my heart—
    And, by the way, my dear, what *was* your name?

BALLADE OF A COMPLETE FLOP

Sad the matter of which I speak,
    Deep the trouble of which I sigh.
To the heavens my woes I shriek—
    I'd just love to sit down and cry.
    Though I hate to admit it, my
Batting av'rage is less than fair.
    Generous gentlemen pass me by—
All that they give me is the air.

Rich man, beggarman, merchant, sheik,
    Actor, congressman, human fly.
Argentinean, Czech, and Greek
    Give and give, till the well runs dry,
    Gifts of elderly Scotch and rye.
Gifts of jewels and orchids rare
    To a more competent Lorelei—
All that they give me is the air.

What's the matter with my technique?
    I can't fathom, or even try.
I'm intelligent, fond, and weak—
    Why don't I get a regular guy?
    Just for others, the goose hangs high;
All love's tokens that form my share
    May be placed in a pig's left eye—
All that they give me is the air.

    L'Envoi
Princes, tell me the reason why.
    What's the trouble, and how, and where?
When did Santa Claus go and die?
    All that they give me is the air.

FOLK SONG

Robin, he is strong and sure,
    Gallant, wise, and gay.
Gavin's heart is calm and pure
    As the new-born day.
Steady shine young Alan's eyes,
    Deep with honesty.
Jack, he tells me naught but lies—
    He's the lad for me.

Richard vows no other maid
    Did he love before.
Will, his beating heart he laid
    At my cottage door.
Peter tells me, "None but you
    Am I thinking of."
Jack, he's wondrously untrue—
    He's my own dear love.

Casper's hair is golden brown;
    Hal is straight and slim.
Martin's richest in the town—
    Who'd say "no" to him?
Rafe's a fine young gentleman;
    Tom's with virtue blest.
Jack, he broke my heart and ran—
    I love him the best.

BALTO

(The Lead Dog of the Team That Brought Antitoxin to Nome)

I think that you could only pity me
      Who'd want to weep and stroke your head and coo
And murmur little names, mellifluously,
      And know no other thing to do.

What should I do, but drop my eyes, and strain
      To cloak the meanness of my offerings,
Who am aggrieved at cold, and hide from pain,
      And live with little, little things.

My days slip by in thin and wavering line;
      Softened my life to such as sick men lead.
And sharp there cuts across dimmed hours like mine
      The cold white radiance of your deed.

Outraging cornered Death, you held the course
      Against the whining night, the whirling day.
When man gave over to the inhuman force,
      Then it was you who led the way.

Though never trumpet urged you to the fight,
      And roystering rush of war was not your part,
Your spirit was a rocket in the night,
      You bore a banner in your heart.

Not hope of cited glory led you then,
      Simply, so went your days since they began.
You did the thing, nor thought of it again,
      A very gallant gentleman.

CASSANDRA DROPS INTO VERSE

We'd break the city's unfeeling clutch
      And back to good Mother Earth we'd go,
With birds and blossoms and such-and-such,
      And love and kisses and so-and-so.
We'd build a bungalow, white and green,
      With rows of hollyhocks, all sedate.
And you'd come out on the five-eighteen
      And meet me down at the garden gate.

We'd leave the city completely flat
      And dwell with chickens and cows and bees,
'Mid brooks and bowers and this and that,
      And joys and blisses and those and these.
We'd greet together the golden days,
      And hail the sun in the morning sky.
We'd find an Eden—to coin a phrase—
      The sole inhabitants, you and I.

With sweet simplicity all our aim,
      We'd fare together to start anew
In peace and quiet and what's-its-name,
      And soul communion, or what have you?
But oh, my love, if we made the flight,
      I see the end of our pastoral plan. . . .
Why, you'd be staying in town each night,
      And I'd elope with the furnace man.

MEETING-PLACE

Here the sky is clear and deep—
    Tedious heart, be gay, be gay!
One and one, like counted sheep,
    Clouds go gamboling away.
(Mary, robed in white and blue,
    Let him swear he has been true.)

Here the leaves are cool and slow—
    Then be quiet, shrieking mind!
And the gracious boughs are low,
    And the roots are sure and kind.
(Lord, that died upon a tree,
    Let him lie, and comfort me.)

SONG OF AMERICANS RESIDENT IN FRANCE

Oh, we are the bold expatriate band!
Allegiance we vow to our chosen land.
How gladly we'd offer our all to France.
We'd give her our honor, our souls, our pants.
We hail her the highest of earthly heavens;
We wriggle our shoulders, and cross our 7's.
With tolerant laughter we rock and sway
Whenever we think of the U.S.A.
At Yankee behavior we writhe and blench.
Our English is rusty—we think in French.
The Sorrows of France disarrange our sleep;
With Gallic abandon we bleed, we weep.
We long to lay down for her all we have;
We love her, we love her, *la belle, la brave!*
We'd see given back to her all her due—
The grandeur, the glory that once she knew.
We'd have her triumphantly hung with flowers,
Acknowledged supremest of all the Powers,
Her dominance written in white and black . . .
But, boy, we'd be sore if the franc came back!

RHYME OF AN INVOLUNTARY VIOLET

When I ponder lovely ladies
Slipping sweetly down to Hades,
Hung and draped with glittering booty—
Am I distant, cold and snooty?
Though I know the price their pearls are
Am I holier than the girls are?
Though they're lavish with their "Yes's,"
Do I point, and shake my tresses?
No! I'm filled with awe and wonder.
I review my every blunder . . .
Do I have the skill to tease a
Guy for an Hispano-Suiza?
I can't even get me taxis
Off to Sydneys, Abes, and Maxies!
Do the pretty things I utter
To the kings of eggs and butter
Gain me pearls as big as boulders,
Clattering, clanking round my shoulders,
Advertising, thus, their full worth?
No, my dear. Mine come from Woolworth.
Does my smile across a table
Win a cloak of Russian sable?
Baby, no. I'd have to kill a
Man to get a near-chinchilla.
Men that come on for conventions
Show me brotherly intentions;
Though my glance be fond and melting,
Do they ever start unbelting

With the gifts they give the others?
No! They tell me of their mothers,
To the baby's pictures treat me,
Say they want the wife to meet me!
Gladly I'd be led to slaughter
Where the ermine flows like water,
When the gay white globes are lighted;
But I've never been invited!
So my summary, in fact, is
What an awful flop my act is!

THE TEMPTRESS

You'd think, with all the age and sense
It has by now, that Providence
Would overlook my vaporings,
And turn its mind to bigger things.
You'd think, compared with flood and war,
My small concerns would be a bore.
But no! The world may go to pot
While I have service no one got.
For do I stretch myself, and smile,
And bask in peace a little while,
And rashly murmur, "Here is bliss"—
It cries, "We must look into this!
Too full her cup to bear a drop;
Well, well, this thing has got to stop."
Or do I weep me harsh and dry,
And raise my futile fists on high,
And curse my dam, and sob, and sweat—
It says, "She ain't seen nothing yet"
(Considering this the latest slang).
So letting all the world go hang,
It sets itself to showing me
What true unhappiness may be.
Ah, could I tempt assorted gents
As sure as I can Providence,
A different story I'd rehearse,
And damned if I'd be writing verse!

TO ELSPETH

Lady, I have read your verse on
Me—the one wherein you write
"How I'd like to meet that person
All alone some ebon night!"

Though your wish to wound were little,
You have done your worst—you see,
Some one, when my heart was brittle,
Said those very words to me.

Lady, take my humble greetings;
Take my thanks; but let me say
Were it not for midnight meetings,
I'd be on my feet to-day.

WHEN WE WERE VERY SORE

*(Lines on Discovering That You Have Been Advertised
as America's A. A. Milne.)*

Dotty had
Great Big
Visions of
Quietude.
Dotty saw an
Ad, and it
Left her
Flat.
Dotty had a
Great Big
Snifter of
Cyanide.
And that (said Dotty)
Is that.

THE ACCURSED

Oh, I shall be, till Gabriel's trump,
Nostalgic for some distant dump;
And ever doomed to weep me dry
For some lost mediocre guy.

CHRIS-CROSS
On Confusing Messrs. Morley and Robin

Christopher Morley goes hippetty, hoppetty,
Hippetty, hippetty, hop.
Whenever I ask him politely to stop it, he
Says he can't possibly stop. . . .

GRANDE PASSION

If you should break your beauteous nose,
My love would perish, I suppose;
Or did your hair go limp and straight,
I might again be celibate.
Were you to slide your step, and peer,
You'd see my little back, I fear;
But lose, my love, your soul and sense—
I should not know the difference.

EXCURSION INTO ASSONANCE

I have trodden level sand
        Along a reach of gray—
From dune-top to sea's end,
        No breathing thing but me.

I have dropped the heavy latch
        Against the rain's tap,
And shivered by the fire, to watch
        The dark hours slip.

The desolate beach, the midnight storm—
        I dwelt alone with these;
But here, within your bended arm,
        Is loneliness.

—AND RETURN

I walked upon a vacant shore
  Beneath a low and thickening sky;
I faced the empty sea, and swore,
  "There is no lonelier one than I."

I waited through a night of lead;
  I heard the showers slide and hiss,
And started at my voice, that said,
  "No loneliness has been but this."

But here, my heart against your own,
  Your petulant kiss to silence me,
I know that I had never known
  How bitter lonely I could be.

SONG OF SOCIAL LIFE IN HOLLYWOOD

One speculates—or doesn't one?
Upon our movie actors' fun;
For it is true as it is right
They don't make pictures all the night.
Now what can there be left, to please
Such fortunates, in hours of ease?
Who labors for his daily bread
Rehearsing scenes would knock you dead
'Mid groves designed, as if by fairies,
For love, and its subsidiaries,
And every lithe and gifted hero
Makes whoopee, *à la mode de* Nero,
With women, wine, and even song,
The livelong day, the live day long—
What's his for fun, when work is through?
What can he do, what DOES he do?
Oh, ask me that, for I have found
There is a rule the world around;
The busman, in his hours of play,
Doth ride a bus, for holiday.

SONNET [2]

In seemly burial, love may not rest;
    A newer love must come to bear away
    The unwanted body of the dead, and lay
The wraith that stalks the heart, a tedious guest.
Let them that knew no fullness go protest
    Their vacant hearts; thus boldly may they say
    That know not haunted night and troubled day.
None who has loved bears now an empty breast.

Weary and waiting, ever on and on,
    Cold love, uncoffined, walks its rut of woe;
Only the live can bid the dead begone—
    The new must come, before the old may go.
And they alone may end the mournful tale
And cry "Farewell!" who first have uttered "Hail!"

LETTER TO OGDEN NASH
Chalet La Bruyere, Montana-Vermala, Switzerland

Dear Sir, I trust you will pardon this intrusion of an Old Subscriber
Who used to dabble for a living in rhyme, as well as vers libre,
But has now Got Away From It All, owing to a plethora of intellectuals,
Racquet Club members, players on two pianos, raconteurs, and
    homosectuals.
I want very much to tell you that were you on an Alp, as I'm,
You would get Ogden Nash's verses though you had to commit arson or
    m'hy'm.
I little thought, at my time of life, to be anxiously awaiting the New Yorker,
(Although I do not buy it, but borrow my friends', thus contributing
    nothing to the stockholders' exchorquer)
But now it's my whitest hope, for I think you are considerably greater
Than Walter Savage Landor, Walter de la Mare, Walter Winchell, and
    Walter Pater,
I wish you all successes, in life as in lit'rature,
And I remain your respectful admirer from the very bottom of my coeur.

AFTER DAWN

Theodore Dreiser
Should ought to write nicer.

SONG IN THE WORST POSSIBLE TASTE

For a Certain Mr. S., Who Got Personal

I shall not see—and don't I know 'em?
A critic lovely as a poem.

OUR COUSINS

Ever I view those people dumbly
Surnamed Mainwaring or Cholmondeley;
Folk at home my sapience staggers
Schooled at Magdalen or Jesus.
Never have I ascertained
Why they all are so refined—
Why aloofness sheds its spell
On the littlest boy or girl—
Why they're stiffer than a bible
On a solid oaken table.
Though I puzzle, make no head I can—
That's for being un-American.

THE PASSIONATE SCREEN WRITER
TO HIS LOVE

Oh come, my love, and join with me
The oldest infant industry.
Come seek the bourne of palm and pearl,
The lovely land of Boy-Meets-Girl,
Come grace this lotus-laden shore,
This Isle of Do-What's-Done-Before.
Come, curb the new, and watch the old win,
Out where the streets are paved with Goldwyn.

THREAT TO A FICKLE LADY

Sweet Lady Sleep, befriend me;
    In pretty mercy, hark.
Your charming manners, tend me—
    Let down your lovely dark.

Sweet lady, take me to you,
    Becalm mine eyes, my breath. . . .
Remember, I that woo you
    Have but to smile at Death. . . .

The
"Hate Verses"

WOMEN
A HATE SONG

I hate Women;
They get on my nerves.

There are the Domestic ones.
They are the worst.
Every moment is packed with Happiness.
They breathe deeply
And walk with large strides, eternally hurrying home
To see about dinner.
They are the kind
Who say, with a tender smile, "Money's not everything."
They are always confronting me with dresses,
Saying, "I made this myself."
They read Woman's pages and try out the recipes.
Oh, how I hate that kind of woman.

Then there are the human Sensitive Plants;
The Bundles of Nerves.
They are different from everybody else; they even tell you so.
Someone is always stepping on their feelings.
Everything hurts them—deeply.
Their eyes are forever filling with tears.
They always want to talk to me about the Real Things,
The things that Matter.
Yes, they know they could write.
Conventions stifle them.
They are always longing to get away—Away from It All!
—I wish to Heaven they would.

And then there are those who are always in Trouble.
Always.
Usually they have Husband-trouble.
They are Wronged.
They are the women whom nobody—understands.
They wear faint, wistful smiles.
And, when spoken to, they start.
They begin by saying they must suffer in silence.
No one will ever know—
And then they go into details.

Then there are the Well-Informed ones.
They are pests.
They know everything on earth
And will tell you about it gladly.
They feel it their mission to correct wrong impressions
They know Dates and Middle names.
They absolutely ooze Current Events.
Oh, how they bore me.

There are the ones who simply cannot Fathom
Why all the men are mad about them.
They say they've tried and tried.
They tell you about someone's husband;
What he said
And how he looked when he said it.
And then they sigh and ask,
"My dear, what is there about me?"
—Don't you hate them?
There are the unfailingly Cheerful ones.
They are usually unmarried.
They are always busy making little Gifts
And planning little surprises.

They tell me to be, like them, always looking on the Bright Side.
They ask me what they would do without their sense of humor?
I sometimes yearn to kill them.
Any jury would acquit me.

I hate Women;
They get on my nerves.

MEN

A HATE SONG

I hate Men;
They irritate me.

I

There are the Serious Thinkers—
There ought to be a law against them.
They see life, as through shell-rimmed glasses, darkly.
They are always drawing their weary hands
Across their wan brows.
They talk about Humanity
As if they had just invented it;
They have to keep helping it along.
They revel in strikes
And they are eternally getting up petitions.
They are doing a wonderful thing for the Great Unwashed—
They are living right down among them.
They can hardly wait
For "The Masses" to appear on the newsstands,
And they read all those Russian novels—
The sex best sellers.

II

There are the Cave Men—
The Specimens of Red-Blooded Manhood.
They eat everything very rare,
They are scarcely ever out of their cold baths,
And they want everybody to feel their muscles.

They talk in loud voices,
Using short Anglo-Saxon words.
They go around raising windows,
And they slap people on the back,
And tell them what they need is exercise.
They are always just on the point of walking to San Francisco,
Or crossing the ocean in a sailboat,
Or going through Russia on a sled—
I wish to God they would!

III
And then there are the Sensitive Souls
Who do interior decorating, for Art's sake.
They always smell faintly of vanilla
And put drops of sandalwood on their cigarettes.
They are continually getting up costume balls
So that they can go
As something out of the "Arabian Nights."
They give studio teas
Where people sit around on cushions
And wish they hadn't come.
They look at a woman languorously, through half-closed eyes,
And tell her, in low, passionate tones,
What she ought to wear.
Color is everything to them—everything;
The wrong shade of purple
Gives them a nervous breakdown.

IV

Then there are the ones
Who are Simply Steeped in Crime.
They tell you how they haven't been to bed
For four nights.
They frequent those dramas
Where the only good lines
Are those of the chorus.
They stagger from one cabaret to another,
And they give you the exact figures of their gambling debts.
They hint darkly at the terrible part
That alcohol plays in their lives.
And then they shake their heads
And say Heaven must decide what is going to become of them—
I wish I were Heaven!

I hate Men;
They irritate me.

ACTRESSES
A HATE SONG

I hate Actresses;
They get on my nerves.

There are the Adventuresses,
The Ladies with Lavender Pasts.
They wear gowns that show all their emotions,
And they simply can't stop undulating.
The only stage properties they require
Are a box of cigarettes and a package of compromising letters.
Their Big Scene invariably takes place in the hero's apartment.
They are always hanging around behind screens
And overhearing things about the heroine.
They go around clutching their temples
And saying, Would to God they were good—
Would to God they were!

There are the Wronged Ones;
The Girls Whose Mothers Never Told Them.
In the first act they wear pink gingham sunbonnets
And believe implicitly in the stork.
In the third act they are clad in somber black
And know that there isn't any Santa Claus.
They are always going out into the night.
They faint a great deal,
And if anyone lets them get near the center of the stage
They immediately burst into hysterics.
They unfortunately never commit suicide until the last act—
It's always the audience that pays and pays and pays.

Then there are the Musical Comedy Stars;
The press-agent's livelihood.
They sing about love—in waltz time—
And they dance as if something were just about to break.
They end by appearing in a piece of court plaster
And an American flag,
And then the audience has to stand up.
The show isn't considered a success
Until they climb into a flower-wreathed swing,
And swing far out, over the orchestra—
Oh, that I might be there when the ropes break.

And there are the Emotional Ones;
The ones who say,
"I'll have two lumps of sugar in my tea, please,"
In exactly the same tones as they say
"Yes, it was I who murdered him."
They are forever tearing their hair—
I hope it hurts them.
They shriek at everything,
Usually at the hero,
And they hurl themselves on the floor at his feet
And say that they wish it were all over—
They said something.

Then there are the child Actresses
Who should be unseen and not heard.
They go around telling people about Heaven
As if they were special correspondents.

They are always climbing up on innocent bystanders
And asking them why they look so sad;
They eternally bring their fathers and mothers together,
Which is always an error of judgment.
They never fail to appear in their nightgowns
And then kneel down beside the orchestra leader,
And say their prayers to the spotlight man—
I wish I were Commodore Gerry.

I hate Actresses;
They get on my nerves.

RELATIVES
A HATE SONG

I hate Relatives;
They cramp my style.

There are Aunts.
Even the best of us have them.
They are always dropping in for little visits,
And when you ask them to stay,
They take it seriously.
They never fail to tell you how badly you look;
And they relate little anecdotes
About friends of theirs who went into Declines.
Their conversation consists entirely of Insides;
They are never out of a Critical Condition.
They are always posing for X-ray portraits
Of parts of their anatomy with names like parlor-cars.
They say the doctor tells them
That they have only one chance in a hundred—
The odds aren't big enough.

Then there are In-Laws,
The Necessary Evils of Matrimony.
The only things they don't say about you
Are the ones they can't pronounce.
No matter what you do,
They know a better way to do it.
They are eternally searching your house for dust;
If they can't find any,
It is a wasted day.
They are always getting their feelings hurt
So that they can go around with martyred expressions
And say that you will appreciate them when they're gone—
You certainly will.

There are Nephews;
They are the lowest form of animal life.
They are forever saying bright things
And there is no known force that can keep them
From reciting little pieces about Our Flag.
They have the real Keystone sense of humor—
They are always firing things off in your ear,
Or pulling away the chair you are about to sit on.
Whenever you are striving to impress anyone,
They always appear
And try out the new words they learned from the ice-man—
I wish the Government would draft all males under ten!

And then there are Husbands;
The White Woman's Burden.
They never notice when you wear anything new—
You have to point it out.
They tell you about the deal they put through,
Or the approach they made,
And you are supposed to get all worked up.
They are always hanging around outside your door
And they are incessantly pulling out watches,
And saying, "Aren't you dressed yet?"
They were never known to be wrong;
Everything is always your fault.
And whenever you go out to have a good time,
You always meet them—
I wish to Heaven somebody would alienate their affections.

I hate Relatives;
They cramp my style.

SLACKERS

A HATE SONG

I hate Slackers;
They get on my nerves.

There are the Conscientious Objectors.
They are the real German atrocities.
They go around saying, "War is a terrible thing,"
As if it were an original line.
They take the war as a personal affront;
They didn't start it—and that lets them out.
They point out how much harder it is
To stay at home and take care of their consciences
Than to go and have some good, clean fun in a nice, comfortable trench.
They explain that it isn't a matter of mere bravery;
They only wish they had the chance to suffer for their convictions—
I hope to God they get their wish!

Then there are the Socialists;
The Professional Bad Sports.
They don't want anybody to have any fun.
If anybody else has more than two dollars,
They consider it a criminal offense.
They look as if the chambermaid forgot to dust them.
There is something about their political views
That makes them wear soiled decolleté shirts,
And they are too full of the spirit of brotherhood
To ask any fellow creature to cut their hair.
They are always telling their troubles to the New Republic;
And are forever blocking the traffic with parades.
If anyone disagrees with them
They immediately go on strike.

They will prove—with a street corner and a soap box—
That the whole darned war was Morgan's fault—
Boy, page an alienist.

There are the Pacifists;
They have chronic stiff necks
From turning the other cheek,
They say they don't believe in war—
As if it were Santa Claus or the Stork.
They will do anything on earth to have peace
Except go out and win it.
Of course they are the only people
Who disapprove of war;
Everybody else thinks it's perfectly great—
The Allies are only fighting
Because it keeps them out in the open air
They know that if we'd all go around wearing lilies,
And simply refusing to fight,
The Kaiser would take his army and go right back home.
It's all wrong, Pershing, it's all wrong.

And then there are the Men of Affairs;
The ones who are too busy to fight.
Business is too good,
And men aren't needed yet, anyway—
Wait till the Germans come over here.
They tell you it would be just their luck
To waste three or four months in a training camp,
And then have peace declared.

It isn't as if they hadn't dependents;
Their wives' relatives can barely buy tires for the Rolls-Royce.
Of course, they may be called in the draft,
But they know they can easily get themselves exempted,
Because they have every symptom of hay fever—
I wish I were head of the draft board!

I hate Slackers;
They get on my nerves.

BOHEMIANS

A HATE SONG

I hate Bohemians;
They shatter my morale.

There are the Artists;
The Inventors of the Nude,
They are always gesticulating with their thumbs,
And sketching, with forks, on table cloths;
They point out all the different colors in a sunset
As if they were trying to sell it to you;
They are forever messing around with batik;
And hanging yellow tassels on things;
And stencilling everything within reach.
I do hope that Gibson never learns what they think of him:
It would simply break his heart.
Of course, they know that being hung in the Academy
Is just a matter of pull.
They say that James Montgomery Flagg may stoop to mere success,
But as for them,
Let them starve first!
Fair enough!

There are the Writers;
The Press Agents for Sex.
They are forever exposing their inmost souls,
Their "stuff" is always "brutally frank"—
Why, they'd just as soon tell you their favorite flower.
They find their fullest expression in free verse;
They call it that
Because they have to give it away.
They are extremely well read,
They can quote from their own works for hours—
Without a mistake.

They are always pulling manuscripts out of their pockets,
And asking you to tell them, honestly—is it too daring?
They would sit down
And write the Great American Novel
If they only could find a publisher Big Enough.
Oh, well—
Genius is an infinite capacity for giving pains.

There are the Actors;
They always refer to themselves as "Players."
Whenever two or three of them are gathered together
Another little theatre comes into the world.
They are eternally leasing vacant kitchenettes
And presenting their own dramas—with Woolworth scenery.
Of course, there can be no real drama above Fourteenth Street.
If they even walked across Times Square
They'd feel that they had lost their amateur standing.
They ask you what you think of their technique,
And then wait for you to commit perjury.
They thank God that they never descended to commercialism;
They know that they'll never be appreciated—
They don't know the half of it.

And then there are the Radicals;
The Table D'Hôte Bolsheviki.
They are always in revolt about something.
Nothing has been done yet that they can wholly approve of.
Their existence is just like Heaven—
There is neither marrying nor giving in marriage.
They are forever starting magazines
And letting the Postal Authorities put the finish to them.

Their one ambition is to get themselves arrested,
So that they can come out and be Heroes.
They are always stifled—
Always longing to loose the trivial fetters of Convention,
And go far away—back to the Real—
I wish they'd get started!

I hate Bohemians;
They shatter my morale.

OUR OFFICE

An Intimate Glimpse of Vanity Fair——En Famille

A HATE SONG

I hate the Office;
It cuts in on my social life.

There is the Art Department;
The Cover Hounds.
They are always explaining how the photographing machine works.
And they stand around in the green light
And look as if they had been found drowned.
They are forever discovering Great Geniuses;
They never fail to find exceptional talents
In any feminine artist under twenty-five.
Whenever the illustrations are late
The fault invariably lies with the editorial department.
They are always rushing around looking for sketches,
And writing mysterious numbers on the backs of photographs,
And cutting out pictures and pasting them into scrapbooks,
And then they say nobody can realize how hard they are worked——
They said something.

Then there is the Editorial Department;
The Literary Lights.
They are just a little holier than other people
Because they can write classics about
" 'Brevity is the soul of lingerie,' said this little chemise to itself";
And "Here are five reasons for the success of the Broadway plays."
They are all full of soul;
Someone is forever stepping on their temperaments.

They are constantly having nervous breakdowns
And going away for a few weeks.
And they only come in on Saturday mornings
To hold the franchise.
They tell you what good training editorial work is.
But they don't mean to stay in it—
Some day they will be Free Lances
And write the Great Thoughts that Surge within them.
They say they only wish they could get away from the office—
That makes it unanimous.

Then there is the Fashion Department;
First Aids to Baron de Meyer.
If any garment costs less than $485
They think you ought to give it to the Belgians.
They look at everything you have on,
And then smile tolerantly
And say, "Sears, Roebuck certainly do a wonderful business, don't they?"
They are forever taking pictures of prominent Wild Women
Dressed as brides and kneeling at Property Altars.
And they write essays on Smart Fashions for Limited Incomes—
The sky's the limit.

There is the Boss;
The Great White Chief.
He made us what we are to-day—
I hope he's satisfied.
He has some bizarre ideas
About his employees' getting to work
At nine o'clock in the morning—
As if they were a lot of milkmen.

He has never been known to see you
When you arrive at 8:45,
But try to come in at a quarter past ten
And he will always go up in the elevator with you.
He goes to Paris on the slightest provocation
And nobody knows why he has to stay there so long.
Oh, well—
You can't expect to keep him down on the farm.

I hate the Office;
It cuts in on my social life.

ACTORS
A HATE SONG

I hate Actors;
They ruin my evenings.

There are the Juveniles;
The Male Ingenues.
They always interpret the rôles of wealthy young sportsmen,
So that they can come running on in white flannels,
Carrying tennis racquets, and wearing spiked shoes.
Whenever the lights go up
They are discovered with their arms around some girl.
They wear their watches and handkerchiefs on their arms,
And they simply couldn't play a scene without their cigarette cases.
They think that the three Greatest Names in American History
Are Hart, Schaffner, and Marx.
They are constantly giving interviews to the Sunday papers
Complaining about the car-loads of mash notes they receive.
They know they have it in them to do something Really Big;
They relate how Belasco told them that they would go far—
I wish they were on their way!

There are the Movie Heroes;
The Boys Who Drove the Wild West Wild.
They are forever fading out into the sunset,
And if they can't pose for a close-up every few feet
They sue the company.
They wear their hair bobbed,
And always look as if they dressed by mail.
They were never known to lose a fight;
The whole troupe of supernumeraries hasn't a chance against them.

They are just bubbling over with animal spirits—
They are continually walking up the side of houses,
Or springing from one galloping horse to another,
Or leaping out of balloons, without parachutes.
And they love to be photographed balancing on one foot
On the extreme edge of the Grand Canyon—
Oh, that I might get behind them, just once!

Then there are the Tragedians;
The Ones Who Made Shakespeare famous.
They are always telling what they used to say to Booth.
And they talk about the old traditions
As if they had collaborated on them.
They make their positively last appearance semi-annually,
And they are just about to go on farewell tour No. 118397, Series H.
They never appear in any rôle
In which they have to wear long trousers.
If they stooped to play in any drama written after 1700,
They know that Art could never be the same.
They are forever striding around the stage in trick tempests,
Wearing aluminum armor, and waving property swords,
And shrieking at Heaven to do its worst—
I wish Heaven would kindly oblige.

And there are the Drawing-Room Stars;
The Ones That Swing a Mean Tea-Cup.
They always appear in those dramas
In which the Big Line is "No cream, please—lemon."
They interpret every emotion
By tapping the left thumb-nail with the cork-tipped cigarette.
They are invariably the best-dressed men on our stage—
Their press-agent says so himself.

They are always standing in the center of the stage
Saying cutting things about marriage;
And they hang around in property moonlight,
Making middle-aged love.
They cherish secret ambitions
To take off their cutaways and play Hamlet:
They know they could be great
If the public would only give them their just due—
If it only would!

I hate Actors;
They ruin my evenings.

BORES

A HYMN OF HATE

I hate Bores;
They take the joy out of my life.

There are the Symptom Collectors.
They have tried every specialist once.
They go about, quoting what they said under ether;
They give readings from their fever-charts;
And they carry their cast-off appendixes with them, in bottles—
Just for old times' sake.
They are forever showing you X-ray photographs
Of their quaint crannies and intimate inglenooks.
They say that you can never guess what they suffer,
And then they clear up all doubts.
Every doctor tells them that their case is hopeless—
I'll say it is.

Then there are the Parlor Comedians.
They have memorized the entire series
Of history's favorite anecdotes.
They begin by saying that they just heard a new one—
Which is the funniest line in the whole story.
They go in strongly for the kind of humor
That requires special apparatus.
They will go miles to procure an exploding cigar
Or a perforated drinking-glass.
They have a repertoire of sure-fire comedy hits:
They address all waiters as "George."
And they love to call you on the telephone
And say, "This is Police Headquarters speaking."
They save up all their witticisms for you,
And tell you how everyone nearly dies at them—
Nearly dies is right.

There are the Gluttons for Business.
They started on a shoe string
And worked their way up to white spats.
They are entirely self-made,
And think that everybody is clamoring for the recipe.
Their life is an open ledger;
They tell you all the inside gossip
About invoices and bills of lading,
And illustrate their talk with diagrams
Showing their increased output throughout the Middle West.
They relate heart-rending stories
Of how they haven't had a vacation in ten years,
And how they wish they could go away for a while—
And I wish they could go away from now on.

And there are the Amateur Mediums.
They are always fooling around with the spirits.
They are constantly receiving messages from the Great Beyond
Saying Uncle Walter is well
And hopes everybody at home is the same.
They spend every night
Being warned, in dreams, of their friends' deaths.
There is nothing that they can't worm out of a ouija board.
They are so messy around the house;
They are always tipping tables
And sitting around in circles, with the lights out.
They are forever seeing things and hearing knocks,
And they just know they have clairvoyant minds—
If any.

I hate Bores;
They take the joy out of my life.

THE DRAMA
A HYMN OF HATE

I hate the Drama;
It cuts in on my sleep.

There is the Clean Play;
The one you take Aunt Etta to see
After a day's sightseeing in the financial district.
The hero is the man from Back Home,
With the blameless life and the creaseless trousers—
A real rough rhinestone.
He may not be so strong on grammar,
But he loves children and sleeping outdoors.
The heroine sneers at him in Act I,
But after he has shown up the effete aristocracy,
And received news that they've struck oil
Back in the Little Marigold well,
She listens to reason.
And when the curtain falls at eleven o'clock,
They are starting out for the Great, Clean West together—
Three hours too late.

Then there is the Comedy of Manners;
The manners provide most of the comedy.
It is all about the goings-on in titled circles—
How Her Grace's handkerchief
Was found in Sir Arthur's diggings.
Tea flows like water,
Butlers are everywhere,
And there is practically no stint to the epigrams
About there being two kinds of husbands:
Your own, and the kind that is in love with you.

Everybody stands about,
Gesticulating with cucumber sandwiches,
And saying, "Oh, Lord Cyril, what a cynic you are!"
There is always a little country ingenue
Who tearfully goes back home in the last act,
Declaring that those society people are all rotten—
She said it.

There is the Farthest North performance
Of the Play That Makes You Think—
Makes you think that you should have gone to the movies.
It is translated from the Norwegian;
They might just as well give it in the original.
All the lighting is dim
So that the actors' faces can scarcely be distinguished,
Which is doubtless all for the best.
The heroine is invariably Misunderstood—
Probably because of her accent.
She is a regular little Glad Girl,
Always falling in love with an innocent bystander,
Or finding that she has married her uncle by mistake,
Or going out into the night and slamming the door.
And things come to a rousing climax
In a nice, restful suicide, or a promising case of insanity.
You tell 'em, Ibsen; you've got the Scandinavian rights.

And there is the Allegorical Drama;
It becomes as sounding brass or a tinkling symbol.
The critics can always find subtle shades of meaning in it—
The triumph of mind over Maeterlinck.

The actors play the parts
Of Light, Joy, Beauty, and Imagination,
While the audience represent Ennui and Bewilderment.
The leading character is searching for Happiness.
And after hunting through four acts, twenty-seven scenes,
And a company of three hundred, exclusive of stage-hands,
He finally discovers it at home—
Would to Heaven he had looked there in the first place!

I hate the Drama;
It cuts in on my sleep.

PARTIES

A HYMN OF HATE

I hate Parties;
They bring out the worst in me.

There is the Novelty Affair,
Given by the woman
Who is awfully clever at that sort of thing.
Everybody must come in fancy dress;
There are always eleven Old-Fashioned Girls,
And fourteen Hawaiian gentlemen
Wearing the native costume
Of last season's tennis clothes, with a wreath around the neck.

The hostess introduces a series of clean, home games:
Each participant is given a fair chance
To guess the number of seeds in a cucumber,
Or thread a needle against time,
Or see how many names of wild flowers he knows.
Ice cream in trick formations,
And punch like Volstead used to make
Buoy up the players after the mental strain.
You have to tell the hostess that it's a riot,
And she says she'll just die if you don't come to her next party—
If only a guarantee went with that!

Then there is the Bridge Festival.
The winner is awarded an arts-and-crafts hearth-brush,
And all the rest get garlands of hothouse raspberries.
You cut for partners
And draw the man who wrote the game.
He won't let bygones be bygones;

After each hand
He starts getting personal about your motives in leading clubs,
And one word frequently leads to another.

At the next table
You have one of those partners
Who says it is nothing but a game, after all.
He trumps your ace
And tries to laugh it off.
And yet they shoot men like Elwell.

There is the Day in the Country;
It seems more like a week.
All the contestants are wedged into automobiles,
And you are allotted the space between two ladies
Who close in on you.
The party gets a nice early start,
Because everybody wants to make a long day of it—
They get their wish.
Everyone contributes a basket of lunch;
Each person has it all figured out
That no one else will think of bringing hard-boiled eggs.

There is intensive picking of dogwood,
And no one is quite sure what poison ivy is like;
They find out by the next day.
Things start off with a rush.
Everybody joins in the old songs,
And points out cloud effects,
And puts in a good word for the color of the grass.

But after the first fifty miles,
Nature doesn't go over so big,
And singing belongs to the lost arts.
There is a slight spurt on the homestretch,
And everyone exclaims over how beautiful the lights of the city look—
I'll say they do.

And there is the informal little Dinner Party;
The lowest form of taking nourishment.
The man on your left draws diagrams with a fork,
Illustrating the way he is going to have the new sun-parlor built on;
And the one on your right
Explains how soon business conditions will be better, and why.

When the more material part of the evening is over,
You have your choice of listening to the Harry Lauder records,
Or having the hostess hem you in
And show you the snapshots of the baby they took last summer.
Just before you break away,
You mutter something to the host and hostess
About sometime soon you must have them over—
Over your dead body.

I hate Parties;
They bring out the worst in me.

MOVIES
A HYMN OF HATE

I hate Movies;
They lower my vitality.

There is the Great Spectacle.
Its press-agent admits
That it is the most remarkable picture ever made.
The story is taken from history,
But the scenario writer smoothes things over a little,
And makes Cleopatra Antony's wife,
Or has Salome marry John the Baptist,
So that you can bring the kiddies.
The management compiles vital statistics
About the size of the cast:
How the entire population of California
Takes part in the battle scenes;
And where the beads worn by the star would reach
If placed end to end.
The audience sits panting
And says, "Think of what it must have cost to produce it!"
Think what could have been saved by not producing it!

Then there is the Picture with Sex Appeal;
The appeal is still unanswered.
The production goes to show
That bad taste, off the screen,
Is still in its infancy.
It seeks to reveal the depths to which society has fallen,
And it proves its point.
It gives glimpses of Night Life in the Great City:
The revelers are shown wearing fancy paper hats,
And marching in lockstep around the table,
And shamelessly performing the two-step.

The characters are always driving home in motors
To the Public Library, or Senator Clark's house.
The interiors are designed
By the man who decorates dentists' waiting-rooms.
The star is a prominent vampire
Who is a nice, sweet girl when she is at home,
And supports an indulgent husband
In the style to which he has become accustomed;
The wages of sin is $3,500 a week.

There is the High Art Production:
They charge three dollars a seat for it—
That's where they get the "high."
The photography is always tricky;
The actors seem to be enveloped in a dense fog,
And that goes for the plot, too.
There is some idea of an allegorical strain running through it,
So that, whenever things are beginning to get good,
And the heroine is just about to fall,
The scene changes
To a panorama of storm clouds,
Or a still-life study of apple blossoms,
Or a view of Hong-Kong harbor by moonlight.
Every few minutes, there is a close-up of the star
Registering one of her three expressions.
The sub-titles offer positive proof
That there is a place where bad metaphors go when they die.
The critics agree unanimously
That the picture removes all doubt
As to whether movies should be classed among the arts—
Removes all doubt is right.

And there is the News of the Week.
It is assembled on the principle
That no news is good news.
It shows all the big events in current history:
The paperweight manufacturers' convention in Des Moines;
The procession of floats during Anti-Litter Week in Topeka;
And the sailors of the U.S.S. Mississippi
Grouped to form the words "E Pluribus Unum."
There is always a view of a wrecked schooner,
Enabling the pianist to oblige with "Asleep in the Deep."
When they have a chance to show a picture of a fire
They color it a mean shade of red.
Before you can get a good look at the event before you,
The scene changes to a new one
Leaving the fate of the people in the last picture hanging—
It's too good for them.

I hate Movies;
They lower my vitality.

BOOKS
A HYMN OF HATE

I hate Books;
They tire my eyes.

There is the Account of Happy Days in Far Tahiti;
The booklet of South Sea Island resorts.
After his four weeks in the South Seas,
The author's English gets pretty rusty
And he has to keep dropping into the native dialect.
He implies that his greatest hardship
Was fighting off the advances of the local girls,
But the rest of the book
Was probably founded on fact.
You can pick up a lot of handy information
On how to serve *poi,*
And where the legend of the breadfruit tree got its start,
And how to take *kava* or let it alone
The author says it's the only life
And as good as promises
That sometime he is going to throw over his writing,
And go end his days with Laughing Sea-pig, the half-caste Knockout—
Why wait?

Then there is the Little Book of Whimsical Essays;
Not a headache in a libraryful.
The author comes right out and tells his favorite foods,
And how much he likes his pipe,
And what his walking-stick means to him—
A thrill on every page.
The essays clean up all doubt
On what the author feels when riding in the subway,
Or strolling along the Palisades.

The writer seems to be going ahead on the idea
That it isn't such a bad old world, after all;
He drowses along
Under the influence of Pollyanesthetics.
No one is ever known to buy the book;
You find it on the guest room night-table,
Or win it at a Five Hundred Party,
Or someone gives it to you for Easter
And follows that up by asking you how you liked it—
Say it with raspberries!

There is the novel of Primitive Emotions;
The Last Word in Unbridled Passions—
Last but not leashed.
The author writes about sex
As if he were the boy who got up the idea.
The hero and heroine may be running wild in the Sahara,
Or camping informally on a desert island,
Or just knocking around the city,
But the plot is always the same—
They never quite make the grade.
The man turns out to be the son of a nobleman,
Or the woman the world's greatest heiress,
And they marry and go to live together—
That can't hold much novelty for them.
It is but a question of time till the book is made into a movie,
Which is no blow to its writer.
People laugh it off
By admitting that it may not be the highest form of art;
But then, they plead, the author must live—
What's the big idea?

And then there is the Realistic Novel;
Five hundred pages without a snicker.
It is practically an open secret
That the book is two dollars' worth of the author's own experiences,
And that if he had not been through them,
It would never have been written,
Which would have been all right with me.
It presents a picture of quiet family life—
Of how little Rosemary yearns to knife Grandpa,
And Father wishes Mother were cold in her grave,
And Bobby wants to marry his big brother.
The author's idea of action
Is to make one of his characters spill the cereal.
The big scene of the book
Is the heroine's decision to make over her old taffeta.
All the characters are in a bad way;
They have a lot of trouble with their suppressions.
The author is constantly explaining that they are all being stifled—
I wish to God he'd give them the air!

I hate Books;
They tire my eyes.

THE YOUNGER SET
A HYMN OF HATE

I hate the Younger Set;
They harden my arteries.

There are the Boy Authors;
The ones who are going to put *belles lettres* on their feet.
Every night before they go to sleep
They kneel down and ask H. L. Mencken
To bless them and make them good boys.
They are always carrying volumes with home-cut pages,
And saying that after all, there is only one Remy de Gourmont;
Which doesn't get any dissension out of me.
They shrink from publicity
As you or I would
From the gift of a million dollars.
At the drop of a hat
They will give readings from their works—
In department stores,
Or grain elevators,
Or ladies' dressing-rooms.
It is pretty hard to get them to show you their work;
Sometimes you even have to ask them to.
They are constantly backing you into corners,
And asking you to glance over some little things
That they just dashed off in a spare year—
Read 'em and weep!

Then there are the Male Flappers;
The Usual Dancing Men.
They can drink one straight Orange Pekoe after another,
And you'd never know that they had had a thing.
Four débutante parties a night is bogie for them,
And their talk is very small indeed.

They never claimed to go so big at a desk,
But they can balance a plate of chicken salad, a cup of bouillon,
And a guest-room-size napkin,
And make gestures with the other hand.
They are mean boys when the orchestra starts;
They work in so many wise steps
That you can't tell whether it's a waltz or a track-meet.
No one can tie them, at a charity entertainment;
They say they have often been told
That with their talent
And the way they can wear clothes
They are simply wasting time on the amateur stage—
I can't give them any argument on that one.

There are the Black Sheep;
The Boys with the Nasty Records.
They are always giving you glimpses of the darker side of life—
Telling you what time they got to bed yesterday morning
And how many people passed out cold,
And where they went from there.
They virtually admit
That if they ever turned over a new leaf
The bootlegging industry would go straight to smash.
They are so inured to alcohol,
That as soon as they've had one cocktail,
They want to go right out and address the Senate.
They are always consulting little red notebooks,
Containing names, telephone numbers, and authors' notes,
And it is an open secret that they have met an actress.
They tell you they know they are going the pace that kills,
And then they laugh bitterly,
And say, "But what does it matter?"—
They took the words right out of my mouth.

And there are the Heavy Thinkers;
The Gluttons for Head-Work.
They have got up a lot of novel ideas
About everybody having a right to live his own life,
And about marriage being just a few words
Muttered over you by a minister.
They say that there may be
Some Supreme Force back of the universe;
They will look into that when they get the time.
Just stand back and give them room,
And they will drop the conventions for the count.
They are pretty low in their minds about America;
They hint that its civilization
Is practically plucking at the coverlet,
And that the Other Side is the only place for intellectuals—
Bon voyage!

I hate the Younger Set;
They harden my arteries.

SUMMER RESORTS

A Hymn of Hate

I hate Summer Resorts;
They ruin my vacation.

There is the Seaside Hotel.
The booklets say that it is right on the water,
And they aren't much over quarter-of-a-mile out of the way.
You are never at a loss for something to do;
You can go down by the waves
And watch the gentleman in sneakers
Trying out his Little Admiral water-wings,
Or you can sit on the porch
And listen to the lady in the next rocker
Explain that this is the first Summer she has ever been to a place
Where the rates were less than fifteen dollars a day.
There is always lots of excitement down on the beach—
Group photographs are constantly being taken.
And posses are being formed to find the person or persons
Who took the garters out of bathhouse number 38
And if you play your cards right,
You may be able to find a dead horseshoe crab.
The more highly-strung guests take you aside and tell you
How much the water means to them.
And how they wish they could stay there beside it for ever and ever—
Good here!

And there is the place where you can get Back to Nature,
Or even farther.
The house was built
When electric lights were regarded as Edison's Folly,
And the surface of plumbing has only been scratched,
And the proprietor hasn't got around to making any changes.

You can tell the tennis court by the net:
Otherwise you would think it was an old-fashioned rock garden
Planted with all the flowers mentioned in Shakespeare's works,
And if you want to play golf,
You will find a course three counties to the left.
The guests are like one big family—
Just like that.
You sit at the table with a lady from Montclair
Who gives talks on the trouble that Junior has had with his tonsils.
Everyone says how restful it all is,
And how it seems as if the city must be a thousand miles away—
It's an under-estimate.

There is the Synthetic Newport;
Luke-warm Dog!
The life is pretty fairly speedy;
Many of the young married set inhale right out in public.
Silver frequently changes hands after the bridge games.
And you'd almost think the cocktails were made of the real stuff—
That goes for the whole works.
Extra-mural affection is generally indulged in:
If you sit down next to your own husband,
It's all over the country club that you are insanely jealous of him.
The revelers have their intellectual side, too;
There is scarcely one of them that hasn't read "The Sheik,"
They are the first to concede that they are hitting things up.
They say that there won't be a thing left of them
If they keep up the pace all Summer—
Stay with 'em, boys!

And then there is the Mountain Resort;
The Home of American Scenery.
You can go yodling up Old Baldy—
Five hundred feet above sea level—
Or you can collect postcard views of Lovers' Leap,
To pass around among your friends on Winter evenings.
You can't conscientiously call it a Summer
Until you get a good, clear day
When you can figure out Washington's profile in the peaks—
You can see a better one on a two-cent stamp
Even when it's raining.
The gossip on the porch keeps you right on the edge of your seat;
One transient tells how he is pretty sure he saw a trout jump,
And hardly has the uproar died down
Before someone else claims to have found some genuine maidenhair fern.
The guests are seldom without a kind word for the landscape,
And they have nothing but praise to offer the air—
It's all theirs.

I hate Summer Resorts;
They ruin my vacation.

WIVES
A HYMN OF HATE

I hate Wives;
Too many people have them.

There are the Splendid Housekeepers;
The Girls Who Shake a Mean Furnace.
Give them a darning-egg, and a box of assorted hooks and eyes,
And they wouldn't change places with Lady Mountbatten.
They keep you right on the edge of your chair
With stories about the stoppage in the kitchen drain,
And how impudent Delia was about those new aprons,
And how they have every reason to believe
That the laundress is taking soap home to her folks.
For comedy relief
They relate how they wise-cracked the butcher
When he told them veal cutlets had gone up.
Their books are their best friends;
They love to browse in "Thirty Pretty Ways to Cook Cauliflower"
Or "Two Hundred Daring Stitches in Filet Crochet."
They can't see why people should want to go out nights;
Their idea of whooping things up
Is to sit by the sewing-table, and listen for Junior's croup.
They are always making second-hand puddings,
Or seeing whether the blue vase doesn't look better on the piano
Than it did on the bookcase.
Oh, well—
It keeps them out of the open air.

Then there are the Veteran Sirens;
The Ones Who Are Wedded, but What of It?
They can take their husbands, or let them alone—
But not in the order named.

Any unmarried man above the age of Jackie Coogan
They regard as All Theirs.
They are constantly helping to fix up bachelor apartments,
Or visiting the male sick, with jars of beef tea,
Or picking out oddities in neckwear for their Boy Friends.
If any man they know goes and gets married,
They feel that they have grounds for a breach of promise suit.
They are always talking in low voices over the telephone,
And carefully dropping letters out of their hand-bags,
And going around full of smiling mystery
About where they are having tea.
They say they wish to goodness
They could have a moment to themselves;
They'd give anything if some nice girl would come along
And take some of their admirers off their hands—
Try and get them!

There are the Drooping Lilies;
The Girls Who Could Have Married That Man with All That Money.
They are always parking a secret sorrow,
And you must guess what the unshed tears are all about.
Their husbands may look normal in public,
But they are Little Better than Animals in the home.
You have no idea what they have to put up with—
Their husbands dance with Another Woman
Twice in the same evening,
Or won't read anything but the newspapers,
Or simply refuse to touch spinach in any form.
If they could only bring themselves
To write down what they have been through
It would be the biggest day that Literature ever saw.

Everyone tells them they might have gone on the stage
And become the toast of the town,
Or put the movies on a paying basis,
Or sent the interior decorating business for a loop—
And here they are—yoked to a lot of Clods!
Things may looks pretty black for them now,
But some day,
Some day they know that they will get their due—
I hope to God they will!

And then there are the Regular Little Pals;
More Like Friends than Wives.
They go everywhere with their husbands
Just to hold the franchise.
You find them up at the Polo Grounds
Asking which is the Yankee eleven;
Or on the golf links
Making a fifth in a Sunday morning foursome;
Or lending a feminine touch to a poker game—
Going ahead on the idea that a straight is better than a flush.
They are a big help in their husbands' business affairs;
They are always dropping in at the office
For little surprise visits.
They smile happily at you
And ask you what their husbands would ever do without them—
I'll give you three guesses!

I hate Wives;
Too many people have them.

HUSBANDS

A HYMN OF HATE

I hate Husbands;
They narrow my scope.

There are the Home Bodies;
The Boys for Whom the Marriage Idea Was Got Up.
If it wasn't for them
The suburbs would have shut down long ago.
Give them a hammer and a mouthful of tacks,
And you'll never have to worry about where they spend their evenings.
Their business cuts in horribly on their night life:
They can hardly wait to rush back to the love nest
And do their stuff.
Some big undertaking is always on their minds—
If it isn't bobbing the hedge,
It's putting up the new shelf for the preserves.
They take you off into corners,
And tell you the latest good one that's going the rounds
About how much they saved by chopping the kindling wood themselves.
They are seldom mistaken for Rudolph Valentino;
The militia has not yet been called out to keep the women back.
They dress right up to their rôle;
The neckties launder without a scruple,
The collars were designed when Gramercy Square was considered up-town,
And the suits were tailored by the visiting seamstress.
It isn't as if they never burned up the White Lights;
Every wedding anniversary
They shoot the works
And take the wife to dinner at Ye Golden Glow Waffle Shoppe.
They are always trying to sell matrimony to the old school friends.
Their big contention is
That there's nothing like it—
Where's the argument?

Then there are the He-Men;
The Masters in Their Own Homes.
The news about the equality of the sexes
Hasn't got around to them yet.
Their conception of the perfect woman
Is one who sews the buttons on before they come off.
They wouldn't give Helen of Troy a second look
If they heard she wasn't so snappy at darning socks.
They are the life of the household;
If the eggs are done longer than three minutes,
They don't speak until the next month.
If the helpmate is ten minutes late getting home
She has to show a letter from her pastor.
They are great boys on a party;
Any time any one else asks the wife to dance,
They want to plead the Unwritten Law.
Their notion of feminine repartee
Is "Yes, dear, of course you're right."
They say that if things ever got to the point
Where they were not the acknowledged Head of the House,
They would never show their faces again—
That's an idea, too.

There are the Steppers-Out;
Married, but What's That between Friends?
They tell you that the wife is a great little woman,
And that closes the subject.
They show you how tall Junior is with one hand,
And try to guess your weight with the other.
Their conquests are a dark secret;
They don't tell a soul until after they have been introduced
They are always looking for new talent;

Can they help it if the rumor got out
That all the last year's Follies Girls
Are so many withered violets to them?
They may always be found on dance floors
Tiring out the flappers;
Or in dark corners
Telling fortunes by palmistry;
Or leaning up against tea tables,
Crazed with cinnamon toast.
Try to tell them what devils they are,
And all the thanks you get for it
Is their lifelong friendship.
They may be a bit gay,
But there is no more harm in them
Than there is in Mussolini.
They explain that some temperaments can stand restraint,
But as for them,
Give them liberty or give them death—
I wish to God they'd leave the decision with me!

And then there are the Gloom Kings;
The Gluttons for Sympathy.
They are the human Einstein theories—
Nobody at home understands them.
They have a rough time getting their stuff across;
The wife may be all very well in her way,
But when it comes to Understanding,
She can't make the grade.
If only they had married some rising young mind-reader,
They could have saved themselves a lot of trouble.
They wear cynical little smiles,
And go around giving impersonations of Disillusionment.

They tell you that of course they can never say anything,
But sometimes they almost think you know—
Which is a big estimate.
You can see that they wish the wife all the luck in the world
By the way they relate the plans for what they would do
If they were ever free.
They like to toy with the idea
That they will just drop quietly Out of Things some day;
They laugh bitterly,
And say everybody would be better off if they did—
The ayes have it!

I hate Husbands;
They narrow my scope.

COLLEGE BOYS
A HYMN OF HATE

I hate College Boys;
They get under my feet.

There are the Boy Butterflies;
The Haberdashers' Livelihood.
Society would be on the rocks without them;
They are as much a part of every tea
As the watercress sandwiches.
They list all the débutantes
In Grades A, B, and C,
And proceed accordingly.
Once they get into their stride,
The Opposite Sex hasn't a prayer.
They are great boys in the moonlight,
And if there were ever a contest in sitting out dances
They could enter at scratch.
They are always dropping lavender envelopes,
Or returning photographs,
Or leaving word that they are not at home
In case a woman's voice asks for them on the telephone.
They wish to God the girls would leave them alone—
That falls right in with my plans.

Then there are the Athletes;
All Full of Red Blood, or What Have You?
They eat their meat just this side of raw,
They are constantly flinging windows open,
And they can hardly wrench themselves out of their cold showers.
They may be the Biceps Kings,
But if you sneak up on them suddenly,
And ask them who discovered America,
They have to rack their memories.

They are all due to make a big name in the business world;
Look at the way they can tear telephone books in half,
And bend silver quarters,
And chin themselves seventy-five consecutive times.
When football comes into the conversation,
It turns out that they are the boys who wrote the rules.
They are always doing something helpful—
You find them on the bathing beaches
Forming human pyramids;
Or on country club verandas
Holding rocking-chairs out at arm's length;
Or standing on their hands
In some lucky girl's parlor.
It's rough that they have to be cramped up in cities;
Way up in the clean, cold, silent out-of-doors,
That's where they ought to be—
And now!

There are the Hot Puppies;
The High-Place Hitters.
They may be young as years go,
But they are old in night life.
You would never dream of the wicked things that go on
If they didn't take pity
And clear it all up for you.
They have piled up a nasty record for themselves;
Try and hear it without blushing.
They tear the town wide open
Until nearly eleven o'clock at night,
They talk right back to policemen.
And when it comes to alcohol,
They imply that they can take it or let it alone—
Reading from left to right.

They concede that they are just about as scarlet as they come,
And they perform a mean laugh,
And say that terrible isn't the word for them—
I heard different.

And there are the Heavy Thinkers;
The Boys That Know the Answers.
Bring up any subject at all
And they'll be glad to set you right on it.
I forget what they go to college for:
It can't be education,
Because they had all that under control years ago.
They don't go so big on a dance floor,
But when the party gets loose,
And Greek irregular verbs are being bandied about,
They are the hit of the evening.
They can hold their audiences spellbound;
If it isn't the latest trigonometry problem that's going the rounds,
Then it's the good one the boys are telling
About the advantages of the parliamentary form of government.
If they were to appear in public
Without a book under their arm
They would feel as if they had come out without their socks.
They seldom hear, when they are spoken to;
It's because their heads are so full
Of little gems of old-world philosophy—
You know the old crack:
Nietzsche abhors a vacuum.

I hate College Boys;
They get under my feet.

Index of First Lines

242

The Complete Chronology

*T*his is a chronological list of *all* of Dorothy Parker's poems and verses. Most of these originally appeared in magazines or newspapers and were later collected in one of four books: *Enough Rope* (*Rope*), *Sunset Gun* (*Gun*), *Death and Taxes* (*Taxes*), and this collection *Not Much Fun* (*Fun*). In some instances the titles were altered when they were collected. Most of the poems that appeared in the first three collections were later compiled in *Not So Deep as a Well* (*Well*). The full contents of *Well*, and one addition, were reprinted in *The Portable Dorothy Parker*. Therefore, excepting that one addition, the *Portable* is not listed here: any poem that is contained in *Well* also appears in the *Portable*.

The chronology follows this format:

Original title [collected title, if different] (Collection, Compilation), then original publication, date, page

Any Porch (*Fun*)	Vanity Fair, September 1915, 32
The Bridge Fiend (*Fun*)	Vanity Fair, January 1916, 118
A Musical Comedy Thought (*Fun*)	Vanity Fair, June 1916, 126
The Gunman and the Débutante (*Fun*)	Vanity Fair, October 1916, 120
The Lady in Back (*Fun*)	Vogue, November 15, 1916, 128
Oh, Look—I Can Do It, Too (*Fun*)	Vanity Fair, December 1918, 48
Letter to Robert Benchley (*Fun*)	Unpublished, September 1920
Our Own Home Talent (*Fun*)	Life, September 30, 1920, 527
With Best Wishes (*Fun*)	Life, December 2, 1920, 1039
Invictus (*Fun*)	Life, February 3, 1921, 160
Song of the Open Country (*Fun*)	Life, April 7, 1921, 487
The Passionate Freudian to His Love (*Fun*)	Life, April 28, 1921, 596
Love Song (*Fun*)	Life, June 30, 1921, 933
Idyl (*Fun*)	Life, July 7, 1921, 3
To My Dog (*Fun*)	Life, July 28, 1921, 8
Absence (*Fun*)	Life, August 18, 1921, 1
Lyric (*Fun*)	Life, September 15, 1921, 3
Song for the First of the Month (*Fun*)	Life, October 6, 1921, 3

PEVL: Walter Savage Landor (*Gun, Well*)	Life, June 2, 1927, 13
PEVL: Harriet Beecher Stowe (*Gun, Well*)	Life, June 2, 1927, 13
PEVL: Alfred Lord Tennyson (*Gun, Well*)	Life, June 2, 1927, 13
PEVL: D. G. Rossetti (*Gun, Well*)	Life, June 2, 1927, 13
PEVL: George Sand (*Gun, Well*)	Life, June 2, 1927, 13
PEVL: George Gissing (*Gun, Well*)	Life, June 2, 1927, 13
PEVL: Thomas Carlyle (*Gun, Well*)	Life, June 2, 1927, 13
PEVL: Alfred Dumas and His Son (*Gun, Well*)	Life, June 2, 1927, 13
PEVL: Charles Dickens (*Gun, Well*)	Life, June 2, 1927, 13
The Red Dress (*Gun, Well*)	Life, June 9, 1927, 13
To a Lady, Who Must Write Verse [For a Lady Who Must Write Verse] (*Gun, Well*)	New Yorker, June 18, 1927, 22
Daylight Saving (*Gun, Well*)	New Yorker, July 2, 1927, 26
Story (*Gun, Well*)	Life, July 14, 1927, 15
Pour Prendre Congé (*Gun, Well*)	New Yorker, July 16, 1927, 21
Frustration (*Gun, Well*)	New Yorker, July 23, 1927, 25
The Counsellor [The Counselor; To Newcastle] (*Gun, Well*)	Life, July 28, 1927, 13
The Homebody (*Gun, Well*)	New Republic, August 3, 1927, 282
Godmother (*Gun, Well*)	NY World, August 23, 1927, 13
Bric-a-Brac (*Gun, Well*)	Bookman, September 1927, 33
Bohemia (*Gun, Well*)	New Yorker, September 17, 1927, 25
Landscape (*Gun, Well*)	Bookman, November 1927—271
Songs for the Nearest Harmonica (SFNH):	
Fairy Story [Fable] (*Gun, Well*)	New Yorker, November 12, 1927, 28
SFNH: But Not Forgotten (*Gun, Well*)	New Yorker, November 12, 1927, 28
SFNH: Reuben's Children (*Gun, Well*)	New Yorker, November 12, 1927, 28
SFNH: Incurable (*Gun, Well*)	New Yorker, November 12, 1927, 28
Chris-Cross (*Fun*)	New Yorker, November 12, 1927, 112
Interior (*Gun, Well*)	Nation, November 30, 1927, 598
The Maid-Servant at the Inn (*Gun, Well*)	Bookman, December 1927, 340
The Gentlest Lady (*Gun, Well*)	McCall's, December 1927, 17
SFNH: Wisdom (*Gun, Well*)	New Yorker, January 7, 1928, 21
SFNH: For R. C. B. (*Gun*)	New Yorker, January 7, 1928, 21
SFNH: Penelope (*Gun, Well*)	New Yorker, January 7, 1928, 21
SFNH: Surprise (*Gun, Well*)	New Yorker, January 7, 1928, 21
SFNH: Post-Graduate (*Gun, Well*)	New Yorker, January 7, 1928, 21
Fair Weather (*Gun, Well*)	NY World, January 20, 1928, 13
The Whistling Girl (*Gun, Well*)	NY World, March 15, 1928, 13
The Last Question (*Gun, Well*)	NY World, March 20, 1928, 13
Coda (*Gun, Well*)	NY World, March 22, 1928, 13
SFNH: The Searched Soul (*Gun, Well*)	New Yorker, May 26, 1928, 20

CCSY: Lines on Reading Too Much
Verse [Lines on Reading Too
Many Poets] (*Taxes, Well*) — NY World, June 25, 1930, 11
CCSY: The Apple Tree (*Taxes, Well*) — NY World, June 25, 1930, 11
CCSY: Requiescat (*Taxes, Well*) — NY World, June 25, 1930, 11
The Little Old Lady in Lavender
Silk (*Taxes, Well*) — NY World, August 1, 1930, 11
Take My Vows [Sonnet for the End of
a Sequence] (*Taxes, Well*) — Yale Review, September 1930, 139
For a Woman, Dead Young [Of a
Woman, Dead Young] (*Taxes, Well*) — NY World, September 15, 1930, 11
Ballade of Unfortunate Mammals
(*Taxes, Well*) — NY World, January 8, 1931, 13
Letter to Ogden Nash (*Fun*) — Saturday Review, January 17, 1931, 544
After a Spanish Proverb (*Taxes, Well*) — NY Herald Tribune, March 3, 1931, 26
Ballade of a Talked-Off
Ear (*Taxes, Well*) — NY Herald Tribune, March 26, 1931, 20
My Own (*Taxes, Well*) — NY Herald Tribune, April 21, 1931, 30
The Sea (*Taxes, Well*) — NY Herald Tribune, April 30, 1931, 20
Pastoraliana (P): Sweet Violets
(*Taxes, Well*) — NY Herald Tribune, May 7, 1931, 20
P: Cherry White (*Taxes, Well*) — NY Herald Tribune, May 7, 1931, 20
P: Sanctuary (*Taxes, Well*) — NY Herald Tribune, May 7, 1931, 20
P: In the Meadow (*Taxes*) — NY Herald Tribune, May 7, 1931, 20
P: The Willow (*Taxes, Well*) — NY Herald Tribune, May 7, 1931, 20
After Dawn (*Fun*) — New Yorker, May 30, 1931, 66
Song In the Worst
Possible Taste (*Fun*) — NY Herald Tribune, October 15, 1931, 21
Sight (*Well*) — NY Herald Tribune, April 21, 1932, 15
Our Cousins (*Fun*) — NY Herald Tribune, December 3, 1932, 11
The Lady's Reward (*Well*) — NY Herald Tribune, April 13, 1933, 15
Prisoner (*Well*) — NY Herald Tribune, October 23, 1933, 13
Autumn Valentine (*Well*) — NY Herald Tribune, November 7, 1935, 21
The Passionate Screen Writer to
His Love (*Fun*) — Unpublished 1937
Threat to a Fickle Lady (*Fun*) — New Yorker, March 26, 1938, 20
War Song (*Portable Dorothy Parker*) — New Yorker, March 4, 1944, 22

Women: A Hate Song (*Fun*) — Vanity Fair, August 1916, 61
Men: A Hate Song (*Fun*) — Vanity Fair, February 1917, 65
Actresses: A Hate Song (*Fun*) — Vanity Fair, May 1917, 64
Relatives: A Hate Song (*Fun*) — Vanity Fair, August 1917, 39

Upon hearing of the poet George Crabbe's death in 1832, the British home secretary (and later prime minister) Lord Melbourne declared, "I am always glad when one of these fellows dies, for then I know I have the whole of him on my shelf."

Permissions

Grateful acknowledgment is given to the following:

The publisher and Mr. Silverstein wish to thank the National Association for the Advancement of Colored People for authorizing the use of Dorothy Parker's works.

"Letter to Robert Benchley" courtesy of the Department of Special Collections, Mugar Memorial Library, Boston University.

"Rosemary [1]" Reprinted from *The Saturday Evening Post* © 1922, 1950; "Song [1]" Reprinted from *The Saturday Evening Post* © 1922, 1950; "Grandfather Said It" Reprinted from *The Saturday Evening Post* © 1922, 1950; "Monody" Reprinted from *The Saturday Evening Post* © 1922, 1950; "Somewhat Delayed Spring Song" Reprinted from *The Saturday Evening Post* © 1922, 1950; "Sonnet [1]" Reprinted from *The Saturday Evening Post* © 1922, 1950; "To a Lady" Reprinted from *The Saturday Evening Post* © 1922, 1950; "Rondeau [2]" Reprinted from *The Saturday Evening Post* © 1922, 1950; "Song of the Conventions" Reprinted from *The Saturday Evening Post* © 1922, 1950; "Song [2]" Reprinted from *The Saturday Evening Post* © 1922, 1950; "Ballade of Understandable Ambitions" Reprinted from *The Saturday Evening Post* © 1923, 1950; "Song of a Contented Heart" Reprinted from *The Saturday Evening Post* © 1923, 1950; "Song of the Wilderness" Reprinted from *The Saturday Evening Post* © 1923, 1950; "A Triolet" Reprinted from *The Saturday Evening Post* © 1923, 1950; "Pæan" Reprinted from *The Saturday Evening Post* © 1923, 1950; "Song [3]" Reprinted from *The Saturday Evening Post* © 1923, 1950; "—And Oblige" Reprinted from *The Saturday Evening Post* © 1923, 1950; "Triolet [2]" Reprinted from *The Saturday Evening Post* © 1923, 1950.

The verses "Christopher Morley goes hippetty, hoppetty . . ." ["Chris-Cross"] and "Theodore Dreiser should ought to write nicer" ["After Dawn"] originally appeared in *The New Yorker* under the rubric "Reading and Writing," by Dorothy Parker © 1927, 1931, 1958, 1959 *The New Yorker* Magazine, Inc. (formerly The F-R Publishing Corp.)